D0711296

WALKING IN
HIS FOOTSTEPS

Christoper G. Cross, KHS

For information about Holy Land Pilgrimages with
Christopher Cross go to www.CatholicHolyLand.com

A Pilgrim's Prayer in the Holy Land

Lord Jesus Christ, you were a pilgrim in this Holy Land. Now you lead and guide us on our pilgrimage to the heavenly Jerusalem. As we follow in your footsteps, we ask the grace to keep our eyes on you. Open our hearts that we may find you not only in ancient stones, but in your people and in each other. Let your words be a fire burning within us. Write your Gospel upon our hearts. Give us a spirit of prayer lest we return full of facts but not of grace and love. Lord, teach us to pray in the very land where you taught your disciples so that we may say: Our Father, who art in heaven, hallowed be thy name . . . .

As Pilgrims we have made the decision to "come and see". Jesus said to his disciples when asked where he stayed "Come and you will see" (John 1:39) Phillip told Nathanial to "come and see" when they had told him they had found the one Moses wrote about in the Law and also the Prophets. (John 1:46)

A Pilgrim is someone who goes on a journey in the hope of encountering God, or of meeting God in a new way. There are many sacred places throughout the world frequented by pilgrims seeking to draw closer to God. We come to the Holy Land because it is the place where our faith has its deepest roots. Here are the places where Jesus himself walked and talked, laughed and wept, where he was born, lived, suffered, died, and rose again. These places hold a memory of Jesus which carries an enormous sense of expectation for one seeking a fresh encounter with God.

TABLE OF CONTENTS

Convento di Terra Santa
P.O.Box 23
16100 Nazareth - Israel
Tel: 04 6572501 Fax: 6460203

02 nd - May - 2002

Dear Christopher Cross,

It is with sincere admiration that I offer you congratulations on the completion of your book Walking In His Footsteps. Without a doubt, it will be extremely beneficial to groups and individuals who wish to make the most of their Holy Land pilgrimage. You have drawn upon your wealth of experience leading countless pilgrimages to provide your readers with Bible passages, prayers and spiritual reflections specifically related to each of the many holy sites. I feel this will help the reader reap the most reward from his/her visit to the Holy Land, and attain a higher level of spirituality than can be given by a local tour guide.

Everything the pilgrim needs is right at his/her fingertips, saving him/her from sifting through the Bible to locate appropriate passages and allowing him/her to concentrate on deepening a relationship with our Lord and brother, Jesus Christ. Having been a Holy Land tour guide myself for the past 15 years, I would not hesitate to recommend this one of kind contemplative guidebook to anyone thinking about making a journey to the Holy Lands or to pilgrims who have already been there and wish to relive their trip. Your pictures of the holy sites are exceptional and truly bring out beauty of this holy and blessed land.

Thanks Chris for providing us with this book. Bravo! May God continue to bless you and all the groups that you bring to the Holy Land .

Friar Thomas Tshabalala o.f.m.

Franciscan guide for pilgrims
in Holyland

VII

Published in the USA by:
Christopher G. Cross, KHS
2823 Whitmyer Drive
Niskayuna, New York 12309

Used by permission:
New Catholic Picture Bible Copyright 1993, 1980
Catholic Book Publish Co.
Totowa, NJ

ISBN-10: 0-615-22667-1
ISBN-13: 978-0-615-22667-5

Printed in the United States of America.

Book and cover design by Darlene Swanson of Van-garde Imagery, Inc.

INTRODUCTION

"WE COULD NOT EVEN have begun to seek for God unless He had already found us. When we go to God we do not go to one who hides himself and keeps us at a distance; we go to one who stands waiting for us, and who even takes the initiative by coming to meet us on the road." St. Augustine

In September 1982, I made my first trip to the Holy Land on a pilgrimage with a group from the United States. We only spent 4 nights in Israel, and I still remember the last day in Jerusalem. I got up early that morning around 4:00 AM and I decided to go alone to the Garden of Gethsemane to pray. As I was walking down to theGarden of Gethsemane, I could see the old city in a distance and noticed Jerusalem's ancient walls, the aromas, and sounds. While praying, I heard a rooster crowing off in the distance and immediately this sound brought cold chills to my body. The thought of St.Peter, when he denied Jesus entered my mind for a brief moment. Never in my wildest dreams would I have imagined that I would make over 49 trips to the Holy Land since that time.

When I first started taking groups to Israel, many were relucant about going because they were not sure whether the trip would be truly a Christian Pilgrimage. I reassured them that it truly was a pilgrimage and not a tour. I still recall that on many of the trips after early morning Mass in the Tomb and on Calvary, I started to notice a change in the attitudes of many of the priests, men and women who came with me. Tears began to appear in many of their eyes as we read scripture at the holy sites. I guess you would say they were being touched by God in His special way. I felt so priviledged to be a small part of this whole experience. There were four priests who had the courage to confide in me at the Tel Aviv Airport after their pilgrimage, that they were considering leaving the priesthood before they made this trip. They shared with me that this trip was a life changing experience for them, and they couldn't thank me enough for making all the arrangements. I realized then that God will use us to touch other people. God never calls the equipped; He equips those He calls.

Over the years, I have compiled and written numerous notes, drawings, readings, and reflections, and found it necessary to put them in some order to be used on future trips to the Holy Land. Tour guides have little knowledge about the spiritual aspect of the gospels and bringing a Bible over with you will not help you unless you are a scriptual scholar and have good working knowledge of the exact location of the readings. One of the problems you will experience while traveling in the Holy Lands is the limited time you have to visit each of the holy sites. It seems like there is never enough time to find all the particular readings in the Bible and then reflect on them. I still remember my first trip to Israel. We were on the road to Emmaus, and I was trying to find the scripture reading that pertains to Emmaus. Two days later I found it, but then we were on the road to Jericho. I missed out on a lot of what was said by the tour guide, because I was too busy trying to find this particular scripture reading. In this book, Walking In His Footsteps, I have compiled all the scripture readings for each of the holy sites as well as some very personal reflections and prayers. The short comments, reflections and prayers in the book are not to be taken as a matter of theology, but as personal reflections.

I realized that many of the people who travel to Israel want to experience something special. They are tired of the politics and the economy. They are broken, and they want spirituality, love and understanding. They want to know God still loves them inspite of their shortcomings, that He is united with them in their daily pains. Most pilgrims coming to Israel want to know more about Jesus. They want to see where He was born, where He lived and where He died, and do it in a very special and holy way. They all want to walk in His footsteps.

In this book, I list what I feel are the 10 best areas to visit while in Israel on a 6 to 10 day pilgrimage. Each area consists of several holy sites at different locations. This book has some beautiful professional pictures of the holy sites and drawings so that one can associate a picture with the story, making it easier to fully understand and meditate on the holy scriptures.

Let me first try to describe the difference between a tour and a pilgrimage. There are many are confused about the two. They come to Israel with the expectation of experiencing a pilgrimage, but instead they experience a tour. Many pilgrims go home disappointed because they didn't get a chance to see and experience the things that were so important to their faith. Their itinerary might mention some of the sites that they were going to visit, but when they go to these sites they really don't experience the holy site in both a historical and spiritual way. In a tour, one may visit a holy site like the Holy Sepulchre in Jerusalem and the tour guide will explain the history of the church and roughly what happened there, then move on quickly to the next site. On a pilgrimage, one visits these holy places with an attitude of experiencing and reading the scriptures that pertains to these holy sites. A short reflection is read describing the readings and their spiritual meaning, concluding with a short prayer. For many who will read this book, scripture come alive for you. You will walk where Jesus walked, see it, feel it and be glad of it.

As we travel along in our spiritual life we continue to have questions about our faith and sometimes these questions are like roadblocks to our spiritual growth. When these questions are answered we can continue our upward spiritual growth toward God. Hopefully, through the use of this book, you may get many of your questions answered about God and how He talks to us through scripture. You will begin to walk in His footsteps.

It is a privilege to share with others the riches God has permitted me to experience. Hopefully, you will enjoy the book as much as I did writing it.

John 1: 25-39

The next day John was there again with two of his disciples, when he saw Jesus walking by. "Here is the Lamb of God!" he said, the two disciples heard him say this and went with Jesus. Jesus turned, saw them following him, and asked, "What are you looking for?" They answered, Where do you live, Rabbi?" "Come and see," he answered so they went with him and saw where he lived, and spend the rest of that day with him.

PRAYER

Tobit 5: 17-18, 21-22 Tobit called his son and said to him: "My son, prepare whatever you need for the journey, and set out with your kinsman. May God in heaven protect you on the way and bring you back to me safe and sound; and may his angel accompany you for safety, my son." Before setting out on his journey, Tobiah kissed his father and mother. Tobit said to him, "Have a safe journey." But his mother began to weep. Tobit

reassured her: "Our son will leave in good health and come back to us in good health. Your own eyes will see the day when he returns to you safe and sound. So, no such thought; do not worry about them, my love. For a good angel will go with him, his journey will be successful, and he will return unharmed." Then she stopped weeping.

CHAPTER 1
CHURCH OF THE HOLY SEPULCHRE
SCRIPTURE READINGS & REFLECTIONS

Tomb of Christ:
Mark 16: 2-4
John 20: 11-18

Calvary
Psalm 145
Luke 23: 35-43
Matthew 27: 27-54
Numbers 21: 4-9
Philippians 2: 6-11
John 3: 13-17

Map of Palestine in time of Christ

Information
about the Tomb

THERE ARE SEVERAL excellent scholars who are working in and around the Church of the Holy Sepulcher, and they are turning up some interesting facts and arguments. Dr. Jerome Murphy-O'Connor, O.P. a Dominican Priest speaking to the Israel Interfaith Association, recently told them that the site of Calvary and the Holy Sepulcher has been traced back to more than a century before the Crucifixion. Back in those pre-Roman days, the site was outside the north walls of Jerusalem and was being used as a quarry.

We're told by St. John that Christ was crucified outside the walls of the city. According to Jewish custom, graves had to be outside the walls as well. Now, we know from previous archaeological excavations that the site of the Church of the Holy Sepulcher was outside the walls through the first third of the first century. It wasn't incorporated into the city until the building of the "Third Wall" by Herod Agrippa in the year 41. That was about 10 years after the Passion.

There are several reasons for believing the church marks the holy sites. When you have a quarry that was abandoned about 100 BC, you have, outside the city, vertical surfaces of bedrock like the walls of a room. So then if you want to dig a burial cave you just go straight in. It's very simple. Otherwise you have to go down and in, a much more complicated process.

That brings us to a question, which St. John also tells us that the Tomb was in a garden. How could this be possible in a quarry?

Well, in a region like this where you have sandstorms, any empty quarry is eventually going to end up with a certain amount of soil. Seeds are wind-blown, and then with a little rain in the winter, you soon have what passes for a garden in this part of the world.

Now, the Romans didn't have in Palestine, at least not in Jerusalem, a regular place of execution. And certainly you would never have had Jewish tombs so close to a place of execution. So Dr. O'Connor's theory is that when the Romans decided to execute Christ, they passed judgment, then said to the centurion on duty, "We'll take him out and do it"! Since on this occasion the charge was that he was claiming to be "King of the Jews," this particular centurion thought it would be the greatest joke in the world to crucify him on what was effectively a rubbish dump.

Fr. O'Connor is a professor of New Testament and inter-testamental literature at the Ecole Biblique in Jerusalem. He believes that the Tomb was never before used, as the Gospels tell us. But he also thinks that it was intended only as a temporary resting place. Jesus was crucified on a Friday, and the disciples had to remove the Body from the cross and place it in a tomb before sunset because of Jewish law. So, they chose the nearest tomb as a temporary resting place. This is, of course, why they went back after the Sabbath, to move the body somewhere else. ...hence the big surprise.

Very interesting, that when you visit the Holy Sepulcher (Church which covers Calvary and the Tomb of Christ) you pass through the main door and immediately on the right side is Calvary. You must pass by Calvary in order to get to the Tomb of Christ. How true this is in our own spiritual life. Whatever ministry you enter, you will have to pass by Calvary in order to get to the Tomb. In other words there will be a certain amount of suffering in each ministry before you get to the resurrection.

Spiritual reading in the Tomb - Resurrection

The joy of Your Resurrection fills our soul with exultation and the realization that our body, too, will rise some day. Like Your Five Wounds, Our suffering will also shine for all to see. The Wisdom of the Father will be glorified forever as all men see how Your plan and Your will in our life mark out the glory that would be ours for all eternity.

All the trials, suffering, heartache, and disappointments will seem as nothing compared to the glory Your sufferings merited for us. They shall all seem like a dream, and the vision of Your face will fill our soul with exquisite joy. Our soul, reunited to our body, will be perfect as Yours is perfect. No evil tendencies will ever again disturb it, no weakness mar its beauty, no separations grieve our soul, no sickness or tears shatter our peace, no regrets cloud our minds. Our memory, like Yours, dear Jesus, will be filled with good things, our intellect will understand the greatest mysteries, our will, ever united to You, will never again experience the pain of rebellion. We will love and be loved by everyone and nothing will be impossible for us. The Father will be ever at our side and together with You, dear Jesus, we will roam freely in the love of the Spirit forever and ever.

Tomb Reading & Prayer

Mark 16: 2-4 And very early in the morning on the first day of the week they went to the tomb when the sun had risen. They had been saying to one another, "Who will roll away the stone for us from the entrance to the tomb?" But when they looked they saw that the stone, which was very big had already been rolled back.

Entrance Christ's Tomb – This is the entrance to the Tomb of Christ, which is located only 165 feet away from Calvary and inside the Holy Sepulchre.

REFLECTION

Where are my stones? What are their names? Would I know them if I met them face-to-face? We all need to be patient with each other's stones. Jesus was gentle with Thomas's stone. Peter had to roll away some stones in his life too. Easter's standing at your door again, so don't we all see that these stones have got to go? That stone of fear, of selfishness, and pride, greed and blindness, and all the other stones we use to keep Jesus in the tomb. We will be racing to the tomb as long as we live. We will be peering into the tomb of our hearts to see if Jesus is really there. Our willingness to remove all stones from the doorways of our tombs is important if we wish to find the hidden life in us.

PRAYER

Jesus, please teach us how to serve you better each day. We don't know what Your destiny will be for each of us, but one thing we do know is that the only ones who will really truly be happy are those who will have sought and found how to serve You. We ask You to give us this strength, perseverance, and courage to continue our ministry in serving others. Amen.

TOMB READING

John 20: 1-9 On the first day of the week, Mary of Magdala came to the tomb early in the morning, while it was still dark, and saw the stone removed from the tomb. So she ran and went to Simon Peter and to the other disciple whom Jesus loved and told them, "They have taken the Lord from the tomb, and we don't know where they put him." So Peter and the other disciple went

out and came to the tomb. They both ran, but the other diciple ran faster than Peter and arrived at the tomb first; he bent down and saw the burial cloths there, but did not go in. When Simon Peter arrived after him, he went into the tomb and saw the burial cloths there, and the cloth that covered his head not with the burial cloths but rolled up in a separate place. Then the other diciple also went in, the one who had arrived at the tomb first, and he saw and believed. For they did not yet understand the Scriptures that He had to rise from the dead.

First century Jewish cemetary showing rolling stone that covers the entrance.

Reflection

No one ever loved Jesus so much as Mary Magdalene. He had done something for her that no one else could ever do, and she could never forget. Mary had sinned much and she loved much, and love was all she had to bring. It was the custom in Palestine to visit the tomb of a loved one for three days after the body had been laid to rest. It was believed that for three days the spirit of the dead person hovered round the tomb, but then it departed because the body had become unrecognizable through decay. Matthew tells us that the authorities had actually sealed the stone to make sure that no one would move it (Matthew 27: 66). Mary was astonished to find it removed. She may have thought that the Jews had taken away Jesus' body, and that not satisfied with killing Him on a cross, they were inflicting further indignities on him. It was a situation Mary felt that she could not face by herself, so she returned to the city to seek out Peter and John. It was Mary, who loved Jesus so much, who was first at the tomb. It was John, the disciple whom Jesus loved and who loved Jesus, who was first to believe in the Resurrection. Love gave John the eyes to read the signs and a mind to understand. In any kind of work it is true that we cannot really interpret the thought of another person, unless between us and him there is a bond of sympathy. We can neither understand Jesus nor help others to understand him unless we take our hearts to him as well as our minds.

John 20: 11-18 Mary stood weeping beside the tomb. Even as she wept, she stooped to peer inside, and there she saw two angels in dazzling robes. One was seated at the head, and the other at the foot of the place where Jesus' body had lain. "Woman," they asked her, "Why are you weeping?" She answered them, "because the Lord has

been taken away, and I do not know where they have put him". She caught sight of Jesus standing there. But she did not recognize him. "Woman," he asked her, " Why are you weeping? Who is it that you are looking for?" She supposed he was the gardener, so she said, "Sir, if you are the one who carried him off, tell me where you have laid him and I will take him away." Jesus said to her, "Mary." She turned to him and said, "Rabbouni" (which means teacher). Jesus then said, "Do not cling to me for I have not yet ascended to the Father. Rather, go to my brothers and tell them I am ascending to my Father and your Father, to my God and your God." Mary Magdalene went to the disciples. "I have seen the Lord," she proclaimed.

REFLECTION-(DO NOT BE AFRAID)

Jesus says to Mary: "Touch me not, for I have not yet ascended to the Father. In just a few more passages, we find Jesus inviting Thomas to touch him. The whole matter has been given a spiritual significance. It has been argued that the only real contact with Jesus does, in fact, come after His Ascension; that it is not the physical touch of hand-to-hand that is important, but the contact that comes through faith with God. Many scholars think what John originally wrote was not "Do not touch me", but "**Do not be afraid**". I haven't gone to my Father yet as I am still here with you. It is not enough for us to see the Lord as Mary did, but better still to actually see Jesus in other people.

CRUCIFIXION OF CHRIST

Matthew 27: 27-54 When they had crucified Him, they divided His clothes among them casting lots; then they sat down there and kept watch over Him. Above His head they had put the charge against him in writing: "THIS IS JESUS, KING OF THE JEWS."

First drawing is a sketch of what Calvary looked like in the time of Christ. Only some 165 feet away was the Tomb. Remember they buried him in a near by Tomb. Golgotha was located outside the city wall.

The Romans filled in the site around Calvary with dirt, which helped to preserve it. They built a Temple to the goddess Venus and tried to discourage Christians from visiting Calvary and the Tomb. Roughly 132-135 AD.

Queen Helena (326 AD) removes the pagan temple to Venus and builds a church on the original site of Golgotha and the Tomb of Christ.

Bottom picture is current picture of entrance to Holy Sepulchre. The Holy Sepulchre covers both Golgotha & the Tomb.

Two insurgents were crucified along with Him, one at his right and one at his left. People going by kept insulting Him, tossing their heads and saying: "So you are the one who was going to destroy the temple and rebuild it in three days! Save yourself, why don't you? Come down off that cross if you are God's Son"! The chief priests, the scribes, and the elders also joined in the jeering: "He saved others but he cannot save himself! So he is the king of Israel! Let's see him come down from that cross and then we will believe in him. He relied on God; let God rescue him now if he wants to. After all, he claimed, "I am God's Son." The insurgents who had been crucified with him kept taunting him in the same way. From noon onward there was darkness over the whole land until mid-afternoon. Then toward mid-afternoon Jesus cried out in a loud tone, " Eli, Eli, lema sabachthani"? That is, "My God, my God, why have you forsaken me?" This made some of the bystanders who heard it remark, "He is invoking Elijah!" Immediately one of them ran off and got a sponge. He soaked it in cheap wine, and sticking it on a reed, tried to make him drink. Meanwhile the rest said, "Leave him alone. Let's see whether Elijah comes to his rescue. Once again Jesus cried out in a loud voice, <u>and then gave up the spirit.</u> (Pause and be silent)

Suddenly the curtain of the sanctuary was torn in two from top to bottom. The earthquake, boulders split, tombs opened. Many bodies of saints who have fallen asleep were raised. After Jesus resurrection they came forth from their tombs ands entered the holy city ands appeared to many. The centurion and his men who were keeping watch over Jesus were terror-stricken at seeing the earthquake and all that was happening, ands said, "clearly this was the Son of God!"

REFLECTION

In human experience, as life goes on and as bitter tragedy enters into it, there come times when we feel that God has forgotten us. We feel we are immersed in a situation beyond our understanding and feel robbed even of God. It may be exactly this that happened to Jesus. He had to go on, because to go on was God's will, and He must accept what even He could not fully understand. The cry of Jesus was from a man who has won through the struggle. It is the cry of the man

The Catholic section of Calvary is in front of the 11th station and to the left of the 12th station is the Altar of our Lady of Sorrows, where the body of Jesus was given to Mary.

who has come out of the dark into the glory of the light, and who has grasped the crown. So, then, Jesus died a victor with a shout of triumph on his lips. The victor is the man who refuses to believe that God has forgotten him, even when every fiber of his being feels that he is forsaken. The victor is the man who has been beaten to the depths and still holds on to God. That is what Jesus did.

In the reading you notice that the Temple veil was torn from top to bottom. That was the veil, which covered the Holy of Holies, that was the veil beyond which no man could penetrate and behind which the Spirit of God dwelt. There is symbolism here. Up to this time God had been hidden and remote, and no man knew what He was like. But in the death of Jesus we see the hidden love of God, and the way to the presence of God, once was barred to all men is now opened to all. The life and the death of Jesus show us what God is like and remove forever the veil, which hid Him from us.

SPIRITUAL READING AFTER COMMUNION MASS ON CALVARY

You loved me enough, dear Jesus, to take upon your bleeding shoulders the wood of Your Cross. My love for You is wanting, for I find physical pain difficult to bear, sorrow oppressive and tragedies cruel. You have asked that I take whatever the Father permits in my life and follow in Your Footsteps, and yet I often think the Cross was meant only for You and not for me. I thought Redemption meant freedom from pain, but I know now, as I see this heavy beam on Your back, that Your Redeeming Cross gives value to my pain. Your footsteps in the coarse ground cushioned the path for my feet. Your Cross cut a ridge in the earth for my cross to rest in. Your Presence cleared the air of hopelessness and then showed me the way. Your acceptance took away the curse and bestowed a blessing. Help me, my Jesus, to carry my cross with joy, ever keeping my eyes on the Father's will. Grant that I may not waste time deciding which cross comes from You and which comes from my neighbor. Let me accept all from You, realizing that some crosses correct me, some release me, some prevent me from a life of sin, others are redemptive, and still others lead to repentance. May our crosses be one cross, dear Jesus, that together we may glorify the Father and save souls. Give us the grace to persevere to the end, and when the journey is over and we have fought the good fight, let the Angels sing the last verse of my earthly song: "**It is finished.**"

Psalm 145 – The Lord is kind and merciful;
slow to anger, and rich in compassion.

WHY DID THIS HAVE TO HAPPEN?

Throughout the Holy Land there are two churches (Church of the Transfiguration, and the Church of the Holy Sepulchre) that have two floors levels to their construction, symbolically showing us the two levels of Jesus (His humanity and His divinity). When we look at Jesus death, we have to consider these two factors and ask the important question, " why"? Why did He have to die this way and for what reason? To further explain this, we have to go back to Genesis, and see how through disobedience we fell out of the graces of God. Or we could say that there was a divine offense committed against God Himself. How could we ever make up for this divine offense? Throughout the Old Testament we see that there were sin offerings made every day, but everything that was offered up was never enough to make up for the divine offense (disobedience). I believe that the only way you make up for a divine offense is to have divine offering. Jesus the Christ was that divine offering. If He wasn't divine, then His death would have never been enough.

Numbers 21: 4-9 From Mount Hor they set out on the Red Sea road, to bypass the land of Edom. But with their patience worn out by the journey, the people complained against God and Moses, "Why have you brought us up from Egypt to die in this desert, where there is no food or water? We are disgusted with this wretched food!" In punishment the Lord sent among the people saraph serpents, which bit the people so that many of them died. Then the people came to Moses and said, "We have sinned in complaining against the Lord and you. Pray the Lord to take the serpents from us." So Moses prayed for the people, and the Lord said to Moses, "Make a saraph and mount it on a pole, and if anyone who has been bitten looks at it, he will recover." Moses accordingly made a bronze serpent and mounted it on a pole, and whenever anyone who had been bitten by a serpent looked at the bronze serpent, he recovered.

Philippians 2: 6-11 Who, though he was in the form of God, did not regard equality with God something to be grasped. Rather He emptied himself, taking the form of a slave, coming in human likeness; and found human in appearance, He humbled himself, becoming obedient to death, even death on a cross. Because of this, God greatly exalted Him and bestowed on him the name that is above every name, that at the name of Jesus every knee should bend, of those in heaven and on earth and under the earth, and every tongue confess that Jesus Christ is Lord, to the glory of God the Father.

John 3: 13-17 No one has gone up to heaven except the one who has come down from heaven, the Son of Man. And just as Moses lifted up the serpent in the desert, so must the Son of Man be lifted up, so that everyone who believes in him may have eternal life.

Sign – King of the Jews – INRI – A fragment of the wooden inscription placed atop the cross on which Jesus was crucified. This relic can be seen in the Church of the Holy Cross of Jerusalem, which is located in Rome, Italy. The original sign was 1 ft. by 3 ft. long and the remaining part after two centuries is now only 6 inches by 18 inches.

REFLECTION

On their journey through the wilderness the people of Israel murmured and complained and regretted that they had ever left Egypt. To punish them God sent a plague of deadly fiery serpents and the people repented and cried for mercy. God instructed Moses to make an image of a serpent and to hold it up in the midst of the camp and those who looked upon the serpent were healed. The Jews themselves were always a little puzzled by this incident in view of the fact that they were absolutely forbidden to make objects of worship made of wood or stone. The rabbis explained it this way: "It was not the serpent that gave life. So long as Moses lifted up the serpent, they believed in Him who had commanded Moses to act this way. It was God who healed them."

When we refer to Jesus being lifted up we refer to a double lifting: Jesus being lifted up upon the Cross, and Jesus being lifted up into glory. The one could not have happened without the other. For Jesus the Cross was the way to glory and had He refused it, had he evaded it, had he taken steps to escape it, as He might so easily have done, there would have been no glory for him. It is the same for us. We can, if we like, choose the easy way, and we can if we like, refusing the cross that every Christian is called to bear; but if we do, we lose the glory. It is an unalterable law of life that if there is no cross, there is no crown or glory. The choice is ours.

CALVARY READING

Luke 23: 35-43 The rulers sneered at Jesus and said, "He saved others, let him save Himself if He is the chosen one, the Christ of God." Even the soldiers jeered at him. As they approached to offer him wine they called out, "If you are King of the Jews, save yourself." Above Him there was an inscription that read, "This is the King of the Jews." Now one of the criminals hanging there reviled Jesus, saying, "Are you not the Christ? Save yourself and us." The other, however, rebuking him, said in reply, "Have you no fear of God, for you are subject to the same condemnation? And indeed, we have been condemned justly, for the sentence we received corresponds to our crimes, but this man has done nothing criminal." Then he said "Jesus, remember me when you come into your kingdom." Jesus replied to him, " Amen, I say to you, today you will be with me in Paradise."

Stone of Unction – Just inside the entrance of the church, is this rock, in the place upon which the body of Jesus was placed, anointed with ointments and wrapped in a linen shroud, the common preparation for burial among Jews.

REFLECTION

There are two important points I would like you to consider. You notice that one thief (Dismas) asked for forgiveness and Jesus granted his request. The good thief died **as a thief** because he stole heaven. You notice that Jesus never rebuked or condemned the other thief, because he always gives us a last chance to ask for forgiveness. Sometimes pride enters our lives and we are too proud to ask God for his forgiveness. Let us all pray that we never become too proud to let God work in our lives, and to ask God to forgive those who don't. Tradition has it that the three Mary's stood near the foot of the cross (Mary Magdeline, Mary the wife of Cleopas, and Mary the Mother of Jesus). They were not allowed to go to the foot of the cross until Jesus was actually up on the cross. Mary approached the foot of the cross and then began her prayer for the two thieves. She wasn't praying for her son because she knew whom her son was and what He had to do, but she was praying for the two thieves. Jesus understood what Mary was doing. It was at this point that Dismas asked Jesus those beautiful words: **when you** enter Your kingdom remember me, not **if you** enter your kingdom. This would indicate that Dismas was given immediate faith, as he truly believed Jesus was the Messiah, and it is my belief that this conversion came as a result of Our Lady's intercession. The second part of the Hail Mary, we ask Mary to pray for us now and at the hour of our death, very much like she did for the Good Thief on the cross. Actually the petition part of the Hail Mary was added as a result of the Nestorian Heresy. We should all pray to Our Lady and ask her to intercede for us as she interceded for the good thief on the cross. Remember that setbacks pave the way for comebacks. Remember that at the moment when Jesus offered Himself to the Father, in His passion and death, mankind's mystical union with Jesus came into being. At that moment Jesus Mystical Body was born. At that moment, even though you were not to be born for many centuries, your own mystical union with Jesus came into existence.

EXALTATION OF THE HOLY CROSS
Celebrated on September 14 Triumph of the Holy Cross

FINDING OF THE HOLY CROSS

The Holy Cross on which Our Lord was crucified was first discovered by **St. Helena**, mother of Constantine the Great, in the year 326. A Roman emperor, Hadrian, about two hundred years before, in order to stop Christians from venerating the mount of Calvary where Jesus was crucified, had raised a large mound of earth over it and dedicated a temple there to the Goddess Venus. When **St. Helena** arrived in Jerusalem, with the help of St. Macarius, Bishop of that city, she had the Temple of Venus destroyed. She hired 200 workmen and 100 soldiers to dig into the ground, and they found the Holy Cross on which Our Lord was crucified. It was identified miraculously by the instantaneous cure of a little boy with a crippled arm and of a woman who was dying.

A large part of the Cross was placed in a church in Jerusalem. The Persians stole this large part of the Cross in the year 615. After many prayers and fasts and a battle to recover it, the Persians were defeated and the Holy Cross was brought back to Jerusalem, 14 years after it was stolen. A large part of the Holy Cross was brought to Rome, and placed in the church called **Holy Cross in Jerusalem**, one of seven great churches located in that city.

Along with finding the True Cross, **St. Helena** also found the nails which were in Jesus' hands and in His feet when he died and the inscription placed above the head of Jesus proclaimed Him in Hebrew, in Greek and in Latin: "Jesus of Nazareth, the King of the Jews". The nails are kept in churches in Europe. One of them is in the Iron Crown of Lombardy. The spear, which pierced Our Lord's side, is kept in one of the pillars of the Vatican in Rome. The inscription over Our Lord's sacred head is kept in the Church of the **Holy Cross-of Jerusalem in Rome. (see attached picture of this historical artifact)** We celebrate the Triumph of the Holy Cross on September 14 each year.

Just a general comment that I found very interesting and something to ponder, and that is the Jews of today still can't believe that one person (Jesus) could have such an impact upon the whole world.

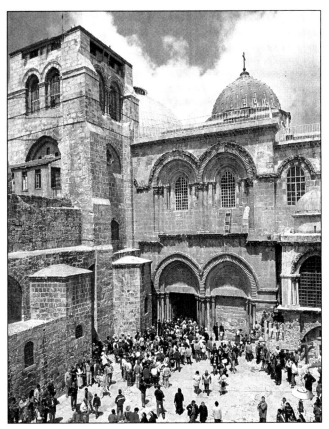

Church of the Holy Sepulchre – Main entrance to the Church of the Holy Sepulchre, which covers both Calvary and the Tomb.

CRUSADERS' CHAPEL

Te Deum Prayer

> You are God: we praise You;
> You are the Lord: we acclaim You;
> You are the eternal Father: All creation worships You.
> To You all angels, all the powers of heaven Cherubim and
>   Seraphim, sing in endless praise: Holy, holy, holy,
>   Lord, God of power and might, heaven and earth are
>   full of your glory.
> The glorious company of apostles praise You. The noble
>   fellowship of prophets praise You. The white-robed
>   army of martyrs praise You.
> Throughout the world the holy Church acclaims You:
>   Father, of majesty unbounded, Your true and only
>   Son, worthy of all worship, and the Holy Spirit,
>   advocate and guide.
> You, Christ, are the king of glory, the eternal Son of the
>   Father.
> When You became man to set us free You did not spurn
>   the Virgin's womb.
> You overcame the sting of death, and opened the kingdom
>   of heaven to all believers.
> You are seated at God's right hand in glory. We believe
>   that You will come, and be our judge. Come then,
>   Lord, and help your people, bought with the price of
>   Your own blood, and bring us with your saints to glory
>   everlasting.

(In addition to its use in the Divine Office, the Te Deum is occasionally said in
Thanksgiving to God for some special blessing. This was the prayer that most of the
crusaders said here in this chapel.)

Chapter 2
Scripture Readings and Reflections

Mosque over the Ascension
Acts 1: 6-13

Pater Noster Church (Our Father Church)
Luke 11:1-4

Panorama View of Jerusalem
Matthew 4: 5-7

Palm Sunday
Luke 19: 28-40

Dominus Flevit (Jesus Weeps over Jerusalem)
Luke 19: 41-44
Matthew 23: 37-39
Mark 13: 3-9

Garden of Gethsemane
Luke 22: 39-53
Luke 22: 47-53

Bethany
Luke 10: 38-42

Lazarus Tomb
John 11: 1-44
John 12: 1-11

Jesus ascends into heaven, higher and higher, until a cloud covers Him and the disciples see Him no longer.

Acts 1: 6-13 When they had gathered together they asked Him, "Lord, are you at this time going to restore the kingdom to Israel?" He answered them, "It is not for you to know the times or seasons that the Father has established by his own authority. But you will receive power when the Holy Spirit comes upon you, and you will be my witnesses in Jerusalem, throughout Judea and Samaria, and to the ends of the earth." When He had said this, as they were looking on, He was lifted up, and a cloud took Him from their sight. While they were looking intently at the sky as He was going, suddenly two men dressed in white garments stood beside them. They said, "Men of Galilee, why are you standing there looking at the sky? This Jesus who has been taken up from you into heaven will return in the same way as you have seen Him going into heaven. Then they returned to Jerusalem from the mount called Olivet, which is near Jerusalem, a Sabbath day's journey away.

Reflection

The apostles were enjoined to wait on the coming of the Holy Spirit. We would gain more power and courage and peace if we learned to wait. In the business of life, we need to learn to be still. "They who wait for the Lord shall renew their strength (Isaiah 40: 31)". Jesus meant a society upon earth where God's will, would be as perfectly done as it is in heaven. Because of that it would be a kingdom founded on love and not on power. We are not to think that the Holy Spirit came into existence now for the first time. It is quite possible for a power always to exist, but for men to experience or take it at some given moment. For instance, we did not invent atomic power. It always existed; but only in our time have we tapped it. So God is eternally Father, Son and Holy Spirit, but there came to men a special time when they experienced to the full that power which had always been present.

Mt. of Ascension – At the top of the Mount of Olives rise a mosque in the place where Jesus rose to heaven, forty days after the Resurrection. This mosque stands upon the ruins of a Byzantine church which already stood here in the 4th century. Saladin remodeled the structure and trannsformed it into a mosque in 1187. Although the site is now under the Muslim control, various Christian denominations are permitted to celebrate the Feast of the Ascension to mark Jesus' ascent to heaven forty days after Easter.

Dear Jesus, I find the day You ascended to the Father a sad day. It resembles my soul when, after experiencing Your Presence, it is plunged into a state of dryness. Like the apostles I tend to stand still and look up in the hope that I will once again experience the joy of Your Presence.

When this happens, my Lord, remind me of the Angel's admonition, "Why do you stand here idle looking up to Heaven?"

This dryness of soul is something I must work **with** and not

against. Help me to realize that when I feel your Presence, You are consoling me, but when I do not feel that Presence and I continue a life of love and virtue, I am consoling You.

Teach me to prefer consoling You to being consoled, and give me the light to exercise my Faith when all seems dark. I want to rise above the demands of my emotions and have the courage to live in spirit and truth. Grant me the **Faith** that is always aware of the invisible reality, the **Hope** that trusts in Your promises, and the **Love** that seeks not itself.

Luke 11: 1-4 One day he was praying in a certain place. When he had finished, one of his disciples asked him, "Lord, teach us to pray, as John taught his disciples." He said to them, " When you pray, say: Father, hallowed be your name, your kingdom come. Give us each day our daily bread. Forgive us our sins for we too forgive all who do us wrong; and subject us not to the trial."

REFLECTION

You notice the first three petitions in the prayer have to do with God and with the glory of God, and the second petitions have to do with our needs and our necessities. God is first given His supreme place, and then, and only then, we turn to ourselves and our needs and desires. The second part of the prayer deals with the three essential needs of man, and the three spheres of time within which man moves. First, we ask for bread, for that which is necessary for the maintenance of life. Second, we ask for forgiveness and thereby bring the past into the presence of God. Third, we ask for help in temptation and thereby commit all the future into the hands of God. In these three brief petitions, we are taught to lay the present, the past, and the future before the footstool of the grace of God. When we ask for bread to

*Legend says this is the Ascension Stone with Jesus
"footprint" in the Dome of the Ascension.*

sustain our earthly lives, that request immediately directs our thoughts to God the Father, the Creator and the Sustainer of all life. When we ask for forgiveness, that request immediately directs our thoughts to God the Son, Jesus Christ our Redeemer. When we ask for help for future temptations, that request immediately directs our thoughts to God the Holy Spirit, the Comforter, the Strengthener and Guardian of our way. The second part of the Lord's Prayer takes the present, the past, and the future, the whole of the man's life, and presents them to God the Father, God the Son and God the Holy Spirit, in all His fullness. The Pater Noster teaches us to bring the whole of life to the whole of God, and to bring the whole of God to the whole of life.

View of the Old City from the Mt. of Olives.

A LORD'S PRAYER FOR JUSTICE
By Ronald Rolheiser

Our Father … who always stands with the weak, the powerless, the poor, the abandoned, the sick, the aged, the very young, the unborn, and those who, by victim of circumstance, bear the heart of the day.

Who art in heaven … where everything will be reversed, where the first will be last and last will be first, but where all will be well and every manner of being will be well.

Hallowed be Thy name… may we always acknowledge your holiness, respecting that your ways are not our ways; your standards are not our standards. May the reverence we give your name pull us out of the selfishness that prevents us from seeing the pain of our neighbor.

Pater Noster Church – Above the ruins of "Eleona" which was built by St. Helena, mother of the Roman Emperor Constantine in the 4th century on the traditional site where Jesus taught his disciples the Lord's Prayer. Around the church are many ceramic panels on which the Lord's Prayer is written in most of the languages of the world.

Your kingdom come …help us to create a world where, beyond our own needs and hurts, we will do justice, love tenderly, and walk humbly with You and each other.

Your will be done …open our freedom to let You in so that the complete mutuality that characterizes Your life might flow through our veins and thus the life that we help generate may radiate your equal love for all and your special love for the poor.

On earth as in heaven …may the work of our hands, the temples and structures we build in this world, reflect the temple and the structure of Your glory so that the joy, graciousness, tenderness, and justice of heaven will show forth within all of our structures on earth.

Give …life and love to us and help us to see always everything as a gift. Help us to know that nothing comes to us by right and that we must give because we have been given to. Help us realize that we must give to the poor, not because they need it, but because our own health depends upon our giving to them.

Us …the truly plural us. Give not just to our own but also to everyone, including those who are very different than the narrow us. Give Your gifts to all of us equally.

This day …not tomorrow. Do not let us push things off into some indefinite future so that we can continue to live justified lives in the face of injustice because we can make good excuses for our inactivity.

Our daily bread …so that each person in the world may have enough food, enough clean water, enough clean air, adequate health care, and sufficient access to education so as to have the sustenance for a healthy life. Teach us to give from our sustenance and not just from our surplus.

And forgive us our trespasses …forgive us our blindness toward our neighbor, our self-preoccupation, our racism, our sexism, and our incurable propensity to worry only about ourselves and our own. Forgive us our capacity to watch the evening news and do nothing about it.

As we forgive those who trespass against us …help us to forgive those who victimize us. Help us to mellow out in spirit, to not grow bitter with age, to forgive the imperfect parents and systems that wounded, cursed, and ignored us.

And do not put us to the test …do not judge us only by whether we have fed the hungry, given clothing to the naked, visited the sick, or tried to mend the systems that victimized the poor. Spare us this test for none of us can stand before Your gospel scrutiny. Give us, instead, more days to mend our ways, our selfishness, and our systems.

But deliver us from evil …that is, from the blindness that lets us continue to participate in anonymous systems within which we need not see who gets less as we get more.
Amen.

Matthew 4:5-7 **Next the devil took him to the holy city, set him on the parapet of the temple, and said, "If you are the Son of God throw yourself down. Scripture has it: he will bid his angels take care of you; with their hands they will support you that you may never stumble on a stone." Jesus answered him, "Scripture also has it: "You shall not put the Lord your God to the test."**

Arial View of Old City & Mt. of Ascension

REFLECTION

Just as metal has to be tested far beyond any stress and strain that it
will ever be called upon to bear, before it can be put to any useful
purpose, so a man has to be tested before God can use him for His
purpose. What we call temptation is not meant to make us sin; it
is meant to enable us to conquer sin. It is not meant to make us
bad, it is meant to make us good. It is not meant to weaken us, it
is meant to make us emerge stronger and finer and purer from the
ordeal. Temptation is not the penalty of being a man; temptation is
the glory of being a man. It is the test, which comes to every man/
woman whom God wishes to use. So we should look at this whole
accident not so much the tempting, as the testing of Jesus.

Luke 19: 28-40 Having spoken thus he went ahead with his ascent to Jerusalem. As he approached Bethpage and Bethany on the mount called Olivet, he sent two of the disciples with these instructions: "Go into the village straight ahead of you. Upon entering it you will find an ass tied there which no one has yet ridden. Untie it and bring it back. If anyone should ask you, "Why are you untying the beast?" say, "The Master has need of it." They departed on their errand and found things just as he had said. As they untied the ass, its owner said to them, "Why are you doing that?" They explained that the Master needed it. Then they led the animal to Jesus, and laying their cloaks on it, helped him mount. They spread their cloaks on the roadway as he moved along, and on his approach to the descent from Mount Olivet, the entire crowd of disciples began to rejoice and praise God loudly for the display of power they had seen, saying: "Blessed be he who comes as king in the name of the Lord! Peace in heaven and glory in the highest." Some of the Pharisees in the crowd said to him. "Teacher, rebuke your disciples". He replied, "If they were to keep silence, I tell you the very stones would cry out."

REFLECTION

Jesus has almost reached his goal. Jerusalem, journey's end, lay just ahead. It was a regular custom for prophets to do something out of the ordinary when people refused to understand their messages. They usually put their message in such fashion that no one failed to see the picture. What Jesus was doing was carefully planned. It was no sudden, impulsive action. Jesus did not leave things until the last moment. The ass in Palestine was not the lowly beast that it is in the United States. It was considered a very noble animal at the time of

*Palm Sunday Route –
The next day a great
crowd who had come to
the feast heard that Jesus
was coming to Jerusalem.
So they took branches
of palm trees and went
out to meet him, crying,
"Hosanna! Blessed is he
who comes in the name of
the Lord. John 12:12-13.*

*Golden Gate – It was through this gate Jesus made his
triumphal entry into Jerusalem on Palm Sunday.*

Christ. Only in war did kings ride upon a horse; when they wanted peace they rode upon an ass. So Jesus, by this action came as a king of love and peace, and not as the conquering military hero whom the mob expected and awaited. Jesus is still inviting us all now to become His sign of peace for everyone. The light you are may be the only light some people ever see.

PRAYER

Blessed are you, God of Israel, so rich in love and mercy. Let these palm branches ever remind us of Christ's triumph. May we who bear them rejoice in his cross and sing your praise forever and ever. Hosanna in the highest.

Mosaic under the altar of Dominus Flevit – This is the site where Jesus wept over Jerusalem, whose destruction he foresaw. "O Jerusalem, Jerusalem, killing the prophets and stoning those who are sent to you! How often would I have gathered your children together as a hen gathers her young under her wings, but you refused me." Matthew 23: 37-38

Church of Dominus Flevit, marking the site where Jesus wept over Jerusalem, whose destruction he foresaw.

Luke 19: 41-44 Coming within sight of the city, he wept over it and said: "If only you had known the path to peace this day; but you have completely lost it from view! Days will come upon you when your enemies encircle you with a rampart, hem you in and press you hard from every side. They will wipe you out, you and your children within your walls, and leave not a stone on a stone within you, because you failed to recognize the time of your visitation."

REFLECTION

Jesus knew what was going to happen to the city. The tragedy was that if only they had abandoned their dreams of political power and taken the way of Christ it would never have happened. How many times have we also rejected God's will in our life and have ended up in tears. The tears of Jesus are the tears of God, when He sees the needless pain and suffering in which men involve themselves through foolish rebelling against His will. How much easier life would be if we could only accept God's will in our own life rather than trying to work against it.

Mark 13: 3-9 and 21-23 As he was sitting on the Mount of Olives, opposite the sacred precincts of the Temple, Peter and James and John and Andrew privately asked Jesus, "Tell us, when shall these things be? Tell us, when will this happen, and what sign will there be when all these things are about to come to an end?" Jesus began to say to them, "See that no one deceives you. Many will come in my name, and say, "I am he, and they will deceive many". When you hear of wars and reports of wars do not be alarmed; such things must happen, but it will not yet be the end. Nations will rise against nation and kingdom against kingdom. There will be earthquakes from place to place and there will be famines. These are the beginnings of the labor pains.

REFLECTION

Jesus was well aware that before the end heretics would arise, and before long the church had its share of heretics. When a man thinks alone he runs a grave danger of thinking astray. There is such a thing as the Tradition of the Holy Church, and there is such a concept as the church being the guardian of truth. If a man finds that his thinking separates himself from the fellowship of men, the chances are that there is something wrong with his thinking. We are all here trying to understand our faith, and this may be one of the reasons you have taken this trip. But because we are finite and God is infinite we can never fully understand. Even at our most intellectual time we must remember that there is a place for the ultimate mystery before which we can only worship, wonder and adore.

Matthew 23: 37-39 O Jerusalem, Jerusalem, murderess of prophets and stoner of those who were sent to you! How often have I yearned to gather your children as a mother hen gathers her young under her wings, but you refused me. Recall the saying, "You will find your temple deserted," I tell you, you will not see me from this time on until you declare, "Blessed is he who comes in the name of the Lord."

REFLECTION

This passage shows several truths, which we all should keep in mind. It shows us the patience of God. Jerusalem had killed the prophets and stoned the messengers of God; yet God did not cast her off, but in the end He sent His Son. It shows us the appeal of Jesus. He will not force an entry, and the only weapon he can use is the appeal of love. It shows us the deliberation of the sin of man. There is no handle on the outside of the door of the human heart; it must be opened from the inside, and sin is the open-eyed, and deliberated refusal of the appeal of God in Jesus Christ. It also shows the consequences of rejecting Christ. Only forty years were to pass and in 70 A.D. Jerusalem would be a heap of ruins. This disaster was a direct consequence of the rejection of Jesus Christ. It is the fact of history even in our time that the nation, which rejects God, is doomed to disaster. If we don't stand for something in our lives we may fall for anything.

PRAYER

God, we pray for our children, growing up in an unsteady and confusing world. Show them that Your ways give more life than the ways of the world, and that following You is better than chasing after selfish goals. Help them to take failure, not as a measure of their worth, but as a chance for a new start. Give them strength to hold their faith in you, and to keep alive their joy in your creation. We ask this through Christ our Lord. Amen

GARDEN OF GETHSEMANE

The Garden of Gethsemane where Jesus went to pray is located in the Kidron Valley, east of the Temple Mount, and only 1 mile from Bethany and Bethpage (Mary and Martha's house). The Judean Desert is only over the hill some 400 yards away. The point that is important was that Jesus could have easily escaped either by going into the Judean Desert or going to Mary and Martha's House. The reason he stayed in the Garden of Gethsemane was the message that He was trying to convey to all of us. It's not the problems in life that matter, but how we react to the problems. During the most difficult time of his agony, Jesus found His answer in prayer and we should too.

Luke 22: 39-53 Then he went out and made his way, as was his custom, to the Mount of Olives; his disciples accompanied him. On reaching the place he said to them. "Pray that you may not be put to the test." He withdrew from them about a stone's throw, then went down on his knees and prayed in these words: "Father, if it is your will, take this cup from me; yet not my will but yours be done." An angel then appeared to him from heaven to strengthen him. In his anguish he prayed with all the greater intensity, and his sweat became like drops of blood falling to the ground. Then he rose from prayer and came to his disciples, only to find them asleep, exhausted with grief. He said to them "Why are you sleeping? Wake up, and pray that you may not be subject to the trial." While he was still speaking a crowd came led by the man named Judas, one of the Twelve. He approached Jesus to embrace him. Jesus said to him, "Judas, would you betray the Son of Man with a kiss?" When the companions of Jesus saw what was going to happen, they said, "Lord, shall we use the sword?" One of them went so far as to strike the slave of the high priest and cut off his right ear. Jesus said in answer to their questions. "Enough!" Then he touched the ear and healed the man. But to those who had come out against him, the chief priests and the temple guard, Jesus said, "Am I a criminal that you come out after me armed with swords and clubs? When I was with you day after day in the temple you never raised a hand against me. But this is your hour, the triumph of darkness!"

REFLECTION

There is no scene like this in all of history. This was the very hinge and turning point in Jesus' life. Whenever we have difficult decisions to make we too must find our answer in prayer.

Agony in the Garden

(The root of Jesse)

Thus says the Lord God: A shoot shall sprout from the stump of Jesse, and from his roots a bud shall blossom. The olive trees in the Garden of Gethsemane continue to grow for thousands of years because a shoot shall sprout from the dead trunk and give the tree new life.

Olive Tree – In the Garden of Gethsemane (which the Aramaic words meaning olive press), there are still eight venerable olive trees, witnesses of the painful agony of the Redeemer. In this garden on the Mount of Olives, Jesus often spent time for prayer and in this garden Jesus underwent the most painful hours of his Passion.

Suffering is an opportunity to absorb more of God into ourselves. In imitation of Jesus we can ask ourselves, who endured the ultimate suffering? Suffering, like death, is a door to God. Christ came to identify with us. He suffered with us. If we suffer, God identifies Himself with us. It is a fact that we do turn more to God when we are in need. Pain can be a good friend, asking you to change. Sometimes, we have to suffer to gain the good things in life. Sometimes we have gone down the wrong path, and God has allowed this thing to happen to show us the way back because we have a free will.

Here we also see Jesus learning the lesson that everyone must someday learn and that is how to accept what you do not understand. Things happen to every one of us in this world that we will not understand, and our faith is sometimes tested to the very limits. Every person has their own Gethsemane and we all have to learn to say like the Blessed Mother said, "Your will be done".

SPIRITUAL MEDITATION

My Jesus, You told Your Apostles many times that You looked forward to the final hour of Redemption, and yet as You foresaw the sufferings to come You shuddered with fear and anguish of soul. You asked the Father to let this chalice pass and You received a refusal. My future looms before me at times, dear Jesus, and I tremble with fear and trepidation. I have implored the Father many times to grant me a favor or release me from a cross and His answer has often been "No". Why should I question His Wisdom in my regard when He refused His own Son because the good of mankind was at stake? Help me to do the Father's Will with Your generosity and to accept a negative reply with Your love. It is the mental anguish and uncertainty that tears my soul apart and I often question His love for me. Your example of resignation, acceptance and love makes me realize that the Father has my life in His hands and nothing happens to me that is not for my good.

Give me the **confidence** to ask for what I think I need, the **humility** to wait for His Will, and the **faith** to accept a refusal. Let my suffering be Redemptive, let my will be one with God's and **my life a sacrifice of love**.

Luke 22: 47-53 While Jesus was still speaking there came a crowd, and the man called Judas, one of the Twelve, was leading them. He came up to Jesus to kiss him, but Jesus said to him, " Judas is it with a kiss that you would betray the Son of Man?" When those

Aerial View of the Garden of Gethsemane – Also known as the Church of All Nations.

Church of Gethsemane – The interior of this church attempts and with great success, to give us a sense of agony. The stone in front of the altar marks the spot where Jesus underwent the most painful hours of his Passion.

Grotto of the Betrayal – This Grotto of the Betrayal is where Jesus and his disciples stayed during their Passover pilgrimage to Jerusalem and to which Judas brought the soldiers and the priests' assistants and betrayed Jesus with a kiss.

who were around him saw what was going to happen, they said, "Lord, shall we strike with the sword?" And one of them struck the servant of the High Priest and cut off his ear. Jesus answered, "Let it come even to this!" Jesus said to the chief priest and the temple captains, and to the elders who had come to him, - "Have you come out with swords and clubs as against a prisoner. When I was daily with you in the Temple you did not lift your hand against me, but this is your hour, and the power of darkness is here."

REFLECTIONS

Judas had found a way to betray Jesus in such a way that the authorities could come upon Him when the crowd was not there. He knew that Jesus was in the habit of going at nights to the garden on the hill, and there he led the emissaries of the Sanhedrin. When a disciple met a beloved Rabbi, he laid his right hand on the Rabbi's left shoulder and kissed him. It was the kiss of a discile to a beloved master that Judas used as a sign of betrayal.

BETHANY & LAZARUS TOMB

Luke 10: 38-42 On their journey Jesus entered a village where a woman named Martha welcomed him to her home. She had a sister named Mary, who seated herself at the Lord's feet and listened to his words. Martha, who was busy with all the details of hospitality, came to him and said, "Lord are you not concerned that my sister has left me to do the household tasks all alone? Tell her to help me."

Jesus answers Martha's complaint, "Only one thing is needful. Mary has chosen the best part, and it will not be taken away from her."

The Lord in reply said to her: "Martha, Martha, you are anxious and upset about many things; one thing only is required. Mary has chosen the better portion and she shall not be deprived of it."

REFLECTION

Here we show a clash of temperaments. We have never allowed enough for the place of temperaments in our religion. Some people are naturally full of activity; others are naturally quiet. It is hard for the active person to understand the person who sits and contemplates. Likewise the person who is devoted to quiet times and meditation is apt to look down on the person who would rather be active. There is no right or wrong in this. God did not make everyone alike. God needs his Mary's and his Martha's, too. Therein lies the difficulty in this reading. So often we want to be kind to people, but we want to be kind, to them in <u>our way</u>; and should it happen that our way is not the necessary way, we sometimes take offense and think that we are not appreciated. If we are trying to be kind the first necessity is to try to see into the heart of the person we desire to help, and then try to forget all our own plans, and to think only of what he or she needs. Jesus loved Martha, and Mary and they in turn loved Him, but when Martha set out to be kind, it had to be her way of being kind, which was really being unkind to him whose heart cried out for quiet time. Jesus loved Mary, and Mary loved him, and Mary understood. The personality of Mary and Martha may be in each of us, and how we handle it makes all the difference.

LAZARUS TOMB

John 11:1-44 There was a certain man named Lazarus who was sick. He was from Bethany, the village of Mary and her sister Martha. (This Mary whose brother Lazarus was sick was the one

*Lazarus Tomb – Two miles east of Jerusalem on the eastern slope of Mount
of Olives, lies the village of Bethany, where Martha, Mary and Lazarus,
friends of Jesus, lived and Jesus raised Lazarus from the dead.
There are twenty-two steps leading down to Lazarus' tomb.*

who anointed the Lord with perfume and dried his feet with her
hair.) The sisters sent word to Jesus to inform him, "Lord, the one
you love is sick," Upon hearing this, Jesus said: "This sickness is
not to end in death; rather it is for God's glory, that through it the
Son of God may be glorified." Jesus loved Martha and her sister

and Lazarus very much. Yet, after hearing that Lazarus was sick, he stayed on where he was for two days more. Finally he said to his disciples, "Let us go back to Judea." "Rabbi," protested the disciples, "With the Jews only recently trying to stone you, you are going back there again?" Jesus answered: Are there not twelve hours of daylight? If a man goes walking by day he does not stumble because he sees the world bathed in light. But if he goes walking at night he will stumble since there is no light in him."

When Jesus arrived in Bethany, he found that Lazarus had already been in the tomb four days. The village was not far from Jerusalem just under two miles, and many Jewish people had come out to console Martha and Mary over their brother. When Martha heard that Jesus was coming she went to meet him, while Mary sat at home. Martha said to Jesus, "Lord, if you had been here, my brother would never have died. Even now, I am sure that God will give you whatever you ask of him." "Your brother will rise again," Jesus assured her. "I know he will rise again," Martha replied, "in the resurrection on the last day." Jesus told her: "I am the resurrection and the life; whoever believes in me, though they should die, will come to life; and whoever is alive and believes in me will never die. Do you believe this?" "Yes, Lord," she replied. " I have come to believe that you are the Messiah, the Son of God: he who is to come into the world." When she had said this she went back and called her sister Mary. "The Teacher is here, asking for you," she whispered. As soon as Mary heard this, she got up and started out in his direction. (Actually Jesus had not yet come into the village but was still at the spot where Martha had met him.) The Jews who were in the house with Mary consoling her saw her get up quickly and go out, so they followed her, thinking she was going to the tomb to weep there. When Mary came to the place where Jesus was, seeing Him, she fell at His feet and said to Him,

"Lord, if You had been here, my brother would never have died."
When Jesus saw her weeping, and the Jews who had accompanied
her also weeping He was troubled in spirit, moved by the deepest
emotions. "Where have you laid him?" he asked. "Lord, come
and see, "they said. Jesus began to weep, which caused the Jews
to remark, " See how much He loved him!" But some said, "He
opened the eyes of that blind man. Why could He not have done
something to stop this man from dying?" Once again troubled
in spirit, Jesus approached the tomb. It was a cave with a stone
laid across it. "Take away the stone, " Jesus directed. Martha, the
dead man's sister, said to him, "Lord, it has been four days now;
surely there will be a stench!" Jesus replied, "Did I not assure you
that if you believed you would see the glory of God displayed?"
They then took away the stone and Jesus looked upward and said,
"Father, I thank You for having heard Me. I know that You always
hear Me, but I have said this for the sake of the crowd, that they
may believe that You sent Me." Having said this He called loudly,
"Lazarus, come out!" The dead man came out, bound hand and
foot with linen strips, His face wrapped in a cloth. "Untie him,"
Jesus told them, "and let him go free."

REFLECTION

Jesus always goes to the Father for help and guidance and knows
that His request will be answered. Jesus told them that He was
the Resurrection and the Life, which was difficult for all of them
to comprehend. Jesus was not talking in terms of physical life, but
talking about one's spiritual life. A man can become so selfish and
insensitive that he is dead to the needs of others. A man can become
so involved in the petty dishonesties and the petty disloyalties of
life that he is dead to honor. A man can become so hopeless that he
becomes spiritually dead. When all things seem hopeless we need to

Mary bathes the feet of Jesus and anoints them with costly perfume.

turn to God and just ask. The problem stems from our **EGO**, which is an acronym for **e**asing **G**od **o**ut. How true this is of all of us as we have all been guilty of easing God out of our own lives.

John 12: 1-11 Six days before Passover Jesus came to Bethany, the village of Lazarus whom Jesus had raised from the dead. There they gave him a banquet, at which Martha served. Lazarus was one of those at the table with him. Mary brought a pound of costly perfume made from genuine aromatic nard, with which she anointed Jesus' feet. The she dried his feet with her hair, and the house was filled with the ointment's fragrance. Judas Iscariot, one of his disciples (the one about to hand him over), protested: "Why was this perfume not sold? It could have brought three hundred silver pieces, and the money have been given to the poor." (He did not say this out of concern for the poor, but because he was a thief. He held the purse, and used to help himself to what was deposited there.) To this Jesus replied, "Leave her alone, let her keep it against the day they prepare me for burial. The poor you always have with you, but me you will not always have." The great crowd of Jews discovered he was there and came out, not only because of Jesus but also to see Lazarus, whom he had raised from the dead. The fact was, the chief priests planned to kill Lazarus too, because many Jews were going over to Jesus and believing in him on account of Lazarus.

REFLECTION

It was something as precious as that which this woman gave to Jesus, and she gave it because it was the most precious thing she had. Love never calculates; love never thinks how little it can decently give; love's one desire is to give to the uttermost limits, and when it has given all it has to give, it still thinks the gift too little. The disciples were anxious to help the poor, but the Rabbis themselves said, "God allows the poor to be with us always, that the opportunities for doing good may never fail." There are some things that we can do at any time, and there are some things that can be done only once. To miss these opportunities to do them then is to miss the opportunity forever. The only tragedy in this life is to miss the lost opportunity to do well. At the end of Jesus' life there was so much bitterness, so much treachery, so much intrigue, so much tragedy that this story shines like a beacon of light in a very dark world. We all need to be beacons of light in this world now. The light we are may be the only light some people every see.

CHAPTER 3
(Temple area, Pool of Bethesda, Way of Cross, Judgment Seat, Damascus Gate)

Temple Area
Luke 2: 22-39 (Presentation)
Luke 2: 41-52 (Finding of the Child Jesus)
John 2: 13-16 (Money Changers)
Luke 18: 904 (Sin of Pride)
John 8: 1-12 – (Woman caught in adultery)
Matthew 23: 1-12 (Respect for God)
Matthew 18: 21-35 (Forgiveness)
Acts 3: 1-10 (Peter Cures Crippled Man)
Luke 16: 19-31 (The Rich Man Who Never Notices)

St. Stephen's Gate
Act 6: 8-10

Pools of Bethesda, Way of the Cross
John 5: 1-15
John 19: 17
John 10: 17-18
History of the Stations of the Cross

Damascus Gate
Acts 9: 1-18 (Paul's Conversion)

Western Wall – This is what remains of the retaining wall of the esplanade
of the Temple following its destruction in the year 70 AD by the Romans.
Jews came here to wail whenever allowed, hence the other name Wailing
Wall. For the Jews all over the world, this is the most sacred place in the world.

PRESENTATION OF OUR LORD

Luke 2:22-39

When the day came to purify them according to the law of
Moses, the couple brought him up to Jerusalem so that he could
be presented to the Lord, for it is written in the law of the Lord,
"Every first born male shall be consecrated to the Lord." They came
to offer sacrifice, "a pair of turtledoves or two young pigeons," in
accord with the dictate in the law of the Lord.

There lived in Jerusalem at the time a certain man named
Simeon. He was just and pious, and awaited the consolation of
Israel, and the Holy Spirit was upon him. It was revealed to him
by the Holy Spirit that he would not experience death until he
had seen the Anointed of the Lord. He came to the temple now,

Presentation of the Child in the Temple

inspired by the Spirit and when the parents brought in the child Jesus to perform for him the customary ritual of the law, he took him in his arms, and blessed God in these words: "Now, Master, you can dismiss your servant in peace; For my eyes have witnessed your saving deed displayed for all the people to see; A revealing light to the Gentiles, the glory of your people Israel." The child's father and mother were marveling at what was being said about him. Simeon blessed them and said to Mary his Mother: "This child is destined to be the downfall and the rise of many in Israel, a sign that will be opposed, and you yourself shall be pierced with a sword, that the thoughts of many hearts may be laid bare." There was a prophetess called Anna. She was the daughter of Phanuel and she belonged to the tribe of Asher. She was far advanced in years. She had lived with her husband ever since seven years after she came to womanhood, and now she was a widow of eighty-four years of age. She never left the Temple and day and night she worshipped with fasting and with prayers. Coming on the scene at this moment, she gave thanks to God and talked about the child to all who looked forward to the deliverance of Jerusalem. When the pair had fulfilled all the prescriptions of the law of the Lord, they returned to Galilee and their own town of Nazareth. The child grew in size and strength, filled with wisdom, and the grace of God was upon Him.

REFLECTION

Anna, a widow old in age, had known sorrow, but had not grown bitter. Sorrow can do one of two things to us. It can make us hard, bitter, resentful, and rebellious against God, or it can make us kinder, softer, and more sympathetic. It all depends how we think of God. If we think of Him as a tyrant we will resent Him. If we think of Him as a Father who loves us, we will have a much more positive view of God. Several things we can learn from Anna. She was old and she had never ceased to hope. Age can take away the youth and strength of our bodies, but age can also do something worse. It can take away the life of our hearts and the hopes that we once had. Anna never ceased to worship. She spent her life in God's house with God's people. We rob ourselves of a priceless treasure when we neglect to be with God. Anna never ceased to pray, and neither should we. Public worship is great, but private prayer is just as satisfying. The years had left Anna without bitterness and in unshakable hope, because day by day she kept her contact with Him who is the source of strength and in whose strength our weaknesses are made perfect. Take time to pray now, because there will be a time in your life, when you won't be able to pray.

PRAYER

O God, You who dwell in unapproachable light, you have come among us to lighten our darkness. Open our eyes to see your glory concealed in the revelations of daily life, and open our hearts to receive you with Simeon's and Anna's welcoming faith. We always ask this through Jesus Christ, your Son, our Lord, who lives and reigns with you and the Holy Spirit, one God forever and ever. Amen.

1ST TEMPLE PERIOD

Book of Ezra 1: 1-6 In the first year of Cyrus, King of Persia, in order to fulfill the word of the Lord spoken by Jeremiah, the Lord inspired King Cyrus of Persia to issue this proclamation throughout his kingdom, both by word of mouth and in writing: "Thus says Cyrus , king of Persia: "All the kingdoms of the earth the Lord, the God of heaven, has given to me, and he has also charge me to build him a house in Jerusalem, which is in Judah. Therefore, whoever among you belongs to any part of his people, let him go up, and may his God be with him! Let everyone who has survived, in whatever place he may have dwelt, be assisted by the people of that place with silver, gold, goods, and cattle, together with free-will offerings for the house of God in Jerusalem.

Then the family heads of Judah and Benjamin and the priests

and Levites – everyone, that is, whom God has inspired to do so
– prepared to go up to build the house of the Lord in Jerusalem.
All their neighbors gave them help in every way, with silver, gold,
goods, and cattle, and with many precious gifts besides all their
free-will offerings. The word of the Lord.

REFLECTION

This reading takes place some 2,500 years to the Kingdom of Persia
(which is present day Iran). Ezra tells the story of the "second
exodus" of the Jewish people, when King Cyrus of Persia issued a
decree allowing the Jews to return to their homeland from Babylon
(which is present day Iraq) where they had been living in exile for
fifty years. It was a long, hard, nine-hundred mile journey back to
Jerusalem. And once they arrived there they faced the difficult task
of rebuilding the temple and the entire city that had been destroyed
by war some fifty years before and left in ruins.

By the grace of God, Ezra was up to the task in leading the
people in physical and spiritual renewal. He led the people to
recommit themselves to God and his law. This is something that
all of us need to do especially while we are here in Jerusalem. Ezra
taught them how they could live out their calling to be a holy
people, and we also have that same calling to be a holy people.

St. Peter the Apostle tells us that we too are "a chosen race,
a royal priesthood, holy nation, God's own people." Like Ezra's
people, we are called to the work of building and renewing. Only
for us the call is to build up the church by living lives of holiness
and by being witnesses of Jesus' redeeming love. Confident that
God is with us, we do our best to be agents of renewal in this
difficult world today in which we live in. Amen.

Uneven Stairs – The excavated stairway leading to the Temple Mount and the likely place where the Presentation of the Child Jesus took place. The temple was destroyed numerous times, but the original stairs remain. The entrance stairs were purposely built uneven so that no one could run into the Temple without falling. Author sitting on the orginal stairs leading up to the Temple.

CANTICLE OF SIMEON

> Lord, now you let your servant go in peace;
> Your word has been fulfilled:
> My own eyes have seen the salvation
> Which you have prepared in the sight of every people:
> A light to reveal you to all nations
> And the glory of your people Israel.
> Glory to the Father, and to the Son, and to the Holy Spirit,
> As it was in the beginning, is now, and will be forever.
> Amen

Historical

In this passage we see Jesus undergoing three ancient ceremonies, which every Jewish boy had to undergo.

Circumcision - Every Jewish boy was circumcised on the eighth day after his birth. So sacred was that ceremony that it could be carried out even on a Sabbath when the law forbade almost every other act, which was not absolutely essential, and on that day a boy received his name.

The Redemption of the First-born- According to the law (Exodus 13:2) every firstborn male, both of human beings and of cattle, was sacred to God. That law may have been a recognition of the gracious power of God in giving human life, or it may even have been a relic of the day when children were sacrificed to the gods. There was a ceremony called the Redemption of the Firstborn (Numbers 18: 16). It is laid down that for the sum of five shekels, the parents could buy back their son from God. The sum had to be paid to the priest. It could not be paid sooner than thirty-one days after the birth of the child.

The Purification After Childbirth - When a woman gave birth to a child, and if it was a boy, the woman was considered unclean for forty days, if the child was a girl, then the mother was considered unclean for eighty days. The mother could go about her household and daily business, but she could not enter the Temple or share in any religious ceremony. At the end of that time she had to bring to the Temple a lamb for a burnt offering and a young pigeon for a sin offering. Offering a lamb was somewhat expensive, so the law provide that if you were poor and you could not afford a lamb then you may bring another pigeon. The offering of the two pigeons instead of the lamb and the pigeon was technically called **The Offering of the Poor**. It was the offering of the poor, which Mary brought. These 3 ceremonies are strange old ceremonies, but all stem from the conviction that a child is a gift of God. Of all God's gifts there is none for which we shall be so accountable as the gift of a child.

FINDING OF CHILD JESUS IN THE TEMPLE

Luke 2: 41-52 Every year his parents used to go to Jerusalem for the feast of the Passover. When he was twelve years of age, they went up according to the customs of the feast, and when they had completed the days of the feast and returned home, the child Jesus stayed on in Jerusalem. His parents were not aware of this. They thought he was in the caravan and when they had gone a day's journey they looked for him amongst their kinsfolk and acquaintances. When they did not find him they turned back to Jerusalem, looking for him all the time. After three days they

SouthView of Old City

found him in the Temple precincts sitting in the middle of the rabbis, listening to them and asking them questions. When they saw him they were amazed. His mother said to him, "Child, why did you do this to us? Your father and I have been looking for you with great anxiety." He said to them, "Why were you looking for me? Did you not know that I must be in my Father's house?" They did not understand the meaning of what he said to them. So he came home with them and went to Nazareth, and he was obedient to them. His mother kept all these things in her heart. And Jesus advanced in wisdom and age and favor before God and man.

Finding of the Child Jesus in the Temple.

Reflection

A Jewish boy became a man when he was twelve years of age. Jesus was very fascinated with the sacred ritual of Passover in the Temple and the holy city.

When his parents started to return to Nazareth, He lingered behind. It was not through any carelessness that his parents missed him. Usually the women in the caravan started out much earlier than the men, because they traveled much slower. The men started later and traveled faster and both would not meet until evening. No doubt Joseph thought he was with Mary, Mary thought that he was with Joseph, and not until evening camp did they miss him. It was the custom during the Passover season for the Sanhedrin to meet in the Public at the temple to discuss religious and theological questions. It was there they found Jesus.

You notice in the passage where Mary says, "Your father and I have been looking for you anxiously". You notice how very gently, but very definitely Jesus takes the name father from Joseph and gives it to God, as he says, "Did you not know, that I must be in my Father's house." At some time Jesus must have discovered his own unique relationship to God. This discovery did not make him proud or look down on his humble parents. He went home with them, and He was obedient to them. He knew His time would come, and He would be ready. Our time will come some day too, and will we be ready?

Jesus Gets Angry in the Temple Money changers

John 2: 13-16 The Passover Feast of the Jews was near, and Jesus went up to Jerusalem. In the Temple he found those who were selling oxen and sheep and doves, and the money-changers sitting at their tables. He made a scourge of cords and drove them all out

of the Temple, and the sheep and oxen as well. He scattered the coins of the exchangers and overturned their tables. He said to those who were selling doves: "Take these away and stop making my Father's house a house of trade."

History of the Temple Tax

In the time of Christ there could be roughly 200,000 Jews visiting Jerusalem during the Feast of Passover. There was Temple Tax, which every Jew over the age of nineteen had to pay before entering the temple. It was necessary that all should pay this Temple Tax. The tax was roughly one/half shekel, which equaled two day's wages. The Temple Tax had to be paid in either Galilaean shekels or in shekels of the sanctuary. The other foreign coins that were used at that time were considered unclean and could never be used to pay the Temple Tax. People would arrive from all over the known world with all kinds of coins. So in the Temple Courts there were money changers. The exchange rate for Temple Coins was at the discretion of the changers and enormous profits were being taken at the expense of those who could ill afford it. The pilgrims were being fleeced at an exorbitant rate by the money changers, and it was a shameless social injustice, and to make matters worse it was being done in the name of religion. Also in the Temple were the sellers of oxen, sheep and doves. Frequently a visit to the Temple meant a sacrifice. But the Jewish law was that any animal offered in sacrifice must be perfect and unblemished. The Temple had authorities who inspected the victims to be offered. There was an inspection fee imposed on all animals. If someone brought an animal from outside the Temple it would normally be rejected after examination. If you bought an animal from those selling inside the Temple (approved inspectors) you would normally pay 5 times the amount you paid on the outside. It was bare-faced extortion at the expense of the poor that moved Jesus to a flaming anger. Just because Jesus loved God, He loved God's children, and it was impossible for Him to stand passively by while the worshippers in Jerusalem were being treated this way. Now you know the story!

THE SIN OF PRIDE

Luke 18: 9-14 Jesus spoke this parable addressed to those who believed in their own self-righteousness while holding everyone else in contempt: "Two men went up to the temple to pray; one was a Pharisee, the other a tax collector. The Pharisee with head unbowed prayed in this fashion: "I give you thanks, O God, that I am not like the rest of men – grasping, crooked, adulterous - or even like this tax collector. I fast twice a week. I pay tithes on all I possess." The other man, however, kept his distance, not even daring to raise his eyes to heaven. All he did was beat his breast and say, "O God, be merciful to me, a sinner." Believe me, this man went home from the temple justified but the other did not. For everyone who exalts himself shall be humbled while he who humbles himself shall be exalted."

REFLECTION

The devout Jew observed prayers three times a day with one being at 9: A.M. then 12:00 noon, and 3:00 P.M. Prayer was offered in the Temple so many went up to the Temple courts to pray and here Jesus tells us about two who went. There was a Pharisee who seemed he was giving himself a testimonial before God. The Pharisee did not really go to pray, but to inform God how good he really was, and then there was the tax collector. He stood far off, and would not even lift his eyes to God. His prayer was humble but simple – "O God, be merciful to me the sinner." It was that heart broken, self-despising prayer which won him acceptance before God. The parable tells us certain things about prayer.

No one who is too proud can truly pray, and no person who despises his fellow human being can truly pray. Let us all remember Jesus message on the Beatitudes. Blessed are the meek, for they will inherit the land. We must constantly remind ourselves that we are one of a great big army of sinning, suffering, sorrowing humanity, all needing God's mercy. We too need to be like the tax collector and say, God be merciful to me the sinner.

PRAYER

God of mercy and compassion, grant us the honesty and courage to beat our breasts beside the humble tax collector rather than blow our own trumpet beside the Pharisee. Forgive us the pride that refuses forgiveness, and we ask this through Christ Our Lord. Amen.

WOMAN CAUGHT IN ADULTERY

John 8: 1-12 Then each went to his own house, while Jesus went to the Mount of Olives. But early in the morning he arrived again in the temple area, and all the people started coming to him, and he sat down and taught them. Then the scribes and the Pharisees brought a woman who had been caught in adultery and made her stand in the middle. They said to him, "Teacher, this woman was caught in the very act of committing adultery. Now in the law, Moses commanded us to stone such women. "So what do you say?" They said this to him, so that they could have some charge to bring against him. Jesus bent down and began to write on the ground with his finger. But when they continued asking him, he straightened up and said to them, "Let the one among you who

is without sin be the first to throw a stone at her." Again he bent down and wrote on the ground. And in response, they went away one by one, beginning with the elders. So he was left alone with the woman before him. Then Jesus straightened up and said to her, "Woman, where are they? Has no one condemned you?" She replied, "No one, sir." Then Jesus said, "Neither do I condemn you. Go, and from now on do not sin anymore".

REFLECTION

When a difficult legal question arose, the natural thing was to take it to a Rabbi for a decision. So the scribes and Pharisees approached Jesus as a Rabbi with a woman taken in adultery. The dilemma in which they sought to put Jesus was this. If He said that the woman ought to be stoned to death, two things followed. First He would lose the name He had gained for love and for mercy and never again would be called the friend of sinners. Second He would come into conflict with the Roman law, for the Jews had no power to pass or carry out the death sentence on anyone. If He said that the woman should be pardoned, it could immediately be said that He was teaching men to break the law of Moses, and that he was condoning and even encouraging people to commit adultery. Then Jesus stooped down and wrote with his finger on the ground. Why did He do this now? He may quite simply have wished to gain time and not be rushed into a decision. He may well have deliberately forced the scribes and Pharisees to repeat their charges, so that, in repeating them they might realize the cruelty of the act. He may have not wanted to look on the faces of the scribes and Pharisees and see the cruelty in their eyes, or see the shame of this woman. This all combined to touch the very heart of Jesus in agony and pity, so that he hid His eyes. The Armenians have translated this passage this way: He himself, bowing his head, was writing with his finger on the earth to declare their sins, and they were seeing their several sins on the stones. The suggestion is that Jesus was writing in the dust the sins of the very men who were accusing the woman. Jesus says those beautiful words to this woman and to each of us. Go, and try your best to sin no more.

Matthew 23: 1-12 Jesus told the crowds and his disciples: "The scribes and the Pharisees have succeeded Moses as teachers; therefore, do everything and observe everything they tell you. But do not follow their example. Their words are bold, but their deeds are few. They bind up heavy loads, hard to carry, to lay on other men's shoulders, while they themselves will not lift a finger to budge them. All their works are performed to be seen. They widen their phylacteries and wear huge tassels. They are fond of places of honor at banquets and the front seats in synagogues, of marks of respect in public and of being called "Rabbi." As to you avoid the title "Rabbi". One among you is your teacher, the rest are learners. Do not call anyone on earth your father. Only one is your father, the One in heaven. Avoid being called teachers. Only one is your teacher, the Messiah. The greatest among you will be the one who serves the rest. Whoever exalts himself shall be humbled, but whoever humbles himself shall be exalted. "

REFLECTION

Here we see the Jewish conviction of the continuity of the faith. God gave the Law to Moses; Moses handed it to Joshua; Joshua transmitted it to the elders; the elders passed it down to the prophets; and the prophets gave it to the Scribes and Pharisees. The whole of the Ten Commandments are based on two great principles. They are based on **reverence**; reverence for God, for God's name, for God's day, for the parents God has given to us. They are based on **respect**; respect for a man's life, for his possessions, for his personality, for his good name, for oneself. It was during this time that religion to the Jews had one fundamental effect. It made their religion a thing of thousands upon thousands of rules and regulations, and therefore it made it an intolerable burden for all those trying to show God both reverence and respect.

HISTORY & TRADITION

The Jewish phylacteries come from the book of Exodus 13: 16 and Deuteronomy 6:4-9, 13-21. In order to fulfill these commandments the Jews wore at prayer, and still wear, what are called phylacteries. They are worn on every day except the Sabbath and special holy days. They are like little leather boxes strapped on one of the wrist, one on the forehead. The one worn on the wrist is a little leather box of one compartment, and inside it there is a parchment roll with the following four passages of scripture written on it – Exodus 13: 1-10; 13: 11-16; Deuteronomy 6: 4-9; 11: 13-21. The Pharisees, in order to draw attention to themselves, not only wore phylacteries, but also wore especially big ones, so that he might demonstrate his exemplary obedience to the Law and his piety. They also wore outside tassels. In Numbers 15: 37-41 and in Deuteronomy 22: 12 we read that God commanded his people to make fringes on the borders of their garments so that when they looked on them they might remember the commandments of God. These fringes were like tassels worn on the four corners of the outer garment. It was easy to make these tassels of especially large size so that they became an excessive display of piety, worn, not to remind a man of the commandments, but to draw attention to himself.

THEME IS FORGIVENESS

Matthew 18: 21-35 Peter came up and asked Jesus, "Lord, when my brother wrongs me, how often must I forgive him? Seven times?" "No," Jesus replied, "not seven times; I say, seventy times seven times. That is why the reign of God may be said to be like a king who decided to settle accounts with his officials. When he began his auditing, one was brought in who owned him a huge amount. As he had no way of paying it, his master ordered him to be sold, along with his wife, his children, and all his property, in payment of the debt. At that the official prostrated himself in homage and said, "My lord, be patient with me and I will pay you back in full." Moved with pity, the master let the official go and wrote off the debt. But when that same official went out he met a fellow servant who owed him a mere fraction of what he himself owed. He seized him and throttled him. "Pay back what you owe." He demanded. His fellow servant dropped to his knees and began to plead with him, "Just give me time and I will pay you back in full." But he would hear none of it. Instead, he had him put in jail until he paid back what he owed. When his fellow servants saw what had happened they were badly shaken, and went to their master to report the whole incident. His master sent for him and said, "You worthless wretch! I canceled your entire debt when you pleaded with me. Should you not have dealt mercifully with your fellow servant, as I dealt with you?" Then in anger the master handled him over to the torturers until he paid back all that he owed. My heavenly Father will treat you in exactly the same way unless each of you forgives his brother from his heart."

REFLECTION

It was Rabbinic teaching that a man must forgive his brother three times. Rabbi Jose Ben Hanina said, "He who begs forgiveness from his neighbor must not do so more than three times." The Biblical proof that this was correct was taken from Amos. In the opening chapters of Amos there is a series of condemnations on the various nations for three transgressions and for four (Amos 1:3,6,9,11). From this it was deduced that God's forgiveness extends to three offences and that he visits the sinner with punishment at the fourth. It was not to be thought that a man could be more gracious than God, so forgiveness was limited to three times. This parable teaches certain lessons which Jesus never tired of teaching. It teaches that lesson which runs through all the New Testament a man must forgive in order to be forgiven. He who will not forgive his fellow men cannot hope that God will forgive him. "Blessed are the merciful," said Jesus, "for they shall obtain mercy" (Matthew 5: 7). No sooner had Jesus taught His men His own prayer, than He went on to expand and explain one petition in it: "For if you forgive men their trespasses, your heavenly Father also will forgive you, but if you do not forgive men their trespasses, neither will your Father forgive your trespasses" (Matthew 6: 14-15). As James had it, "For judgment is without mercy to one who has shown no mercy" (James 2: 13). We must remember that Divine and human forgiveness go hand in hand. We have been forgiven a debt, which is beyond all paying for the sin of man brought about the death of God's own Son, and if that is so, we must forgive others as God has forgiven us, or we can hope to find no mercy.

Prayer: *You know, O Lord, how hard we find it to forgive those who have offended us. Yet you ask us to forgive without restrictions. Make us capable, Lord, of the love you ask of us, for alone we cannot do what you have asked. Help us through Christ our Lord. Amen*

NEAR THE ENTRANCE TO THE TEMPLE - CRIPPLED MAN CURE

Acts 3: 1-10 Once, when Peter and John were going up to the temple for prayer at the three o'clock hour, a man crippled from birth was being carried in. They would bring him every day and put him at the temple gate called "the Beautiful" to beg from the people as they entered. When he saw Peter and John on their way in, he begged them for an alms. Peter fixed his gaze on the man; so did John. "Look at us!" Peter said. The cripple gave them his whole attention, hoping to get something. Then Peter said: "I have neither silver nor gold, but what I have I give you! In the name of Jesus Christ the Nazorean, walk!" Then Peter took him by the right hand and pulled him up. Immediately the beggar's feet and ankles became strong; he jumped up, stood for a moment, then began to walk around. He went into the temple with them – walking, jumping about, and praising God. When the people saw him moving and giving praise to God, they recognized him as that beggar who used to sit at the Beautiful Gate of the temple. They were struck with astonishment – utterly stupefied at what had happened to him.

REFLECTIONS

As has been previously stated, for the devout Jew there were three special hours of prayer: 9 AM, noon, and 3 PM. It was double precious if one could pray in the temple courts. It is very interesting that the apostles kept up the customs in which they had been trained. It was the hour of prayer and Peter and John were going into the Temple to observe it. A new faith had come to them, but they did not use that as an excuse for a license, which broke all laws. They were aware that the new faith and the old discipline could walk hand in hand. In the Middle East it was the custom for beggars to sit at the entrance to a temple or a shrine. Such a place was considered the best of all places because when people are on their way to worship God they are disposed to be generous to their fellow men. Love of man and love of God must ever go hand in hand. We can ask ourselves why have miracles stopped during our life time, but have they stopped? It is the simple fact that any doctor or surgeon can now do things, which in apostolic times would have been regarded as miracles. As one doctor told me, "I bandage the wounds, but God heals them." For all of us there are still many miracles happening each day if we only have eyes to see.

THE RICH MAN WHO NEVER NOTICED

Luke 16:19-31 Jesus said to the Pharisees: "Once there was a rich man who dressed in purple and linen and feasted splendidly every day. At his gate lay a beggar named Lazarus, who was covered with sores. Lazarus longed to eat the scraps that fell from the rich man's table. The dogs even came and licked his sores. Eventually the beggar died, and he was carried by angels to the bosom of Abraham. The rich man likewise died and was buried. From the abode of the dead where he was in torment, he raised his eyes and saw Abraham afar off, and Lazarus resting in his bosom. "He called out, "Father Abraham, have pity on me. Send Lazarus to dip the tip of his finger in water to refresh my tongue, for I am tortured in these flames." "My Child," he replied Abraham, "remember that you were well off in your lifetime, while Lazarus was in misery. Now he has found consolation here, but you have found torment. And that is not all. Between you and us there is fixed a great abyss, so that those who might wish to cross from here to you cannot do so, nor can anyone cross from your side to us." "Father, I ask you, then", the rich man said, "send him to my father's house where

I have five brothers. Let him be a warning to them so that they may not end in this place of torment." Abraham answered, "They have Moses and the prophets. Let them hear them." No, Father Abraham," replied the rich man. "But if someone would only go to them from the dead, then they would repent." Abraham said to him, "If they do not listen to Moses and the prophets, they will not be convinced even if one should rise from the dead."

The poor Lazarus begs for scraps from the rich man's table.

REFLECTION

The rich man feasted in luxury every day, while Lazarus was waiting for the crumbs that fell from the table. In that time there were no knives, forks or napkins. Food was eaten with the hands and, in very wealthy houses, the hands were cleansed by wiping them on hunks of bread, which were then thrown away. That was what Lazarus was waiting for. What was the sin of the rich man? He had not ordered Lazarus to be removed from his gate. He made no objections to his receiving the bread that was flung away from his table. He did not kick him in the passing nor was not deliberately cruel to him. The sin of the rich man was that he never noticed Lazarus, that he accepted him as part of the landscape and simple thought it perfectly natural and inevitable that Lazarus should lie in pain and hunger while he wallowed in luxury. This is a terrible warning that the sin of this rich person was not that he did wrong things, but that he did **nothing** to help those less fortunate. We too must look at our lives and see if we are doing nothing to help those who are suffering or are less fortunate than us.

Prayer: *Lord, let there be more caring and sharing, more healing and helping, and more loving and giving in this world and let it start with me.*

ST. STEPHEN'S GATE

Acts of the Apostles 6: 8-10; 7: 54-59 Stephen was a man filled with grace and power, who worked great wonders and signs among the people. Certain members of the so-called "Synagogue of Roman Freedmen" (that is, the Jews from Cyrene, Alexandria, Cilicia and Asia) would undertake to engage Stephen in debate, but they proved no match for the wisdom and spirit with which he spoke. Those who listened to his words were stung to the heart; they ground their teeth in anger

St. Stephen's Gate – It was near this Gate that St. Stephen was killed.

at him. Stephen meanwhile, filled with the Holy Spirit, looked to the sky above and saw the glory of God, and Jesus standing at God's right hand. "Look"!" he exclaimed, "I see an opening in the sky, and the Son of Man standing at Gods' right hand." The onlookers were shouting aloud, holding their hands over their ears as they did so. Then they rushed at him as one man, dragged him out of the city, and began to stone him. The witnesses meanwhile were piling their cloaks at the feet of a young man named Saul. As Stephen was being stoned he could be heard praying, "Lord Jesus, receive my spirit."

Prayer: *Lord God, whose days are without end and whose mercies beyond counting, keep us mindful that life is short and the hour of death unknown. Let your Spirit guide our days on earth in the ways of holiness and justice, that we may serve you in union with the whole Church, sure in faith, strong in hope, perfected in love. And when our earthly journey is ended like St. Stephen, lead us rejoicing into your kingdom, where you live forever and ever. AMEN*

Pool of Bethesda

John 5: 1-15 Cure on a Sabbath Feast- Later, on the occasion of a Jewish feast, Jesus went up to Jerusalem. Now in Jerusalem by the Sheep Pool there is a place with the Hebrew name Bethesda. Its five porticoes were crowded with sick people lying there blind, lame or disabled (waiting for the movement of the water). There was one man who had been sick for thirty-eight years. Jesus, who knew he had been sick a long time, said when he saw him lying there. "Do you want to be healed?" "Sir," the sick man answered, " I do not have anyone to plunge me into the pool once the water has been stirred up. By the time I get there, someone else has gone in ahead of me." Jesus said to him, "Stand up! Pick up your mat and walk!" The man was immediately cured; he picked up his mat and began to walk. The day was a Sabbath. Consequently, some of the Jews began telling the man who had been cured, "It is the Sabbath, and you are not allowed to carry that mat around." He explained: "It was the man who cured me who told me, " Pick up your mat and walk." "This person who told you to pick it up and walk," they asked, "who is he?" The man who had been restored to health had no idea who it was. The crowd in that place was so great that Jesus had been able to slip away. Later on, Jesus found him in the temple precincts, and said to him: "Remember, now,

At the Pool of Bethesda a crowd of sick, blind, helpless and crippled people waited for the water to rise and bubble. Jesus speaks to the cripple and heals them.

Pool of Bethesda – The cistern found on the grounds are known as the Pool of Bethesda mentioned in the Gospel of John, the place where Jesus cured the man who was paralyzed for 38 years.

you have been cured. Give up your sins so that something worse may not overtake you." The man went off and informed the Jews that Jesus was the one who had cured him.

REFLECTION

The five porticoes stand for the five books of the law. The thirty eight years stand for the thirty-eight years in which the Jews wandered in the desert before they entered the promised land; or for the number of the centuries men had been waiting for the Messiah. The stirring of the waters stands for baptism. There are always deeper truths below the surface and even the simple stories are meant to leave us face to face with eternal things. The law simply said that the Sabbath day must be different from others days and on that day neither a man nor his servants nor his animals must work. The Jews set out thirty-nine different classifications of work, one of which consisted in carrying a burden. Jesus defense was shattering. God did not stop working on the Sabbath day, and neither did he. God never ceases doing, but as it is the property of fire to burn, and snow to chill, so it is the property of God to do. The sun shines; rivers flow; the processes of birth and death go on and on, and the Sabbath as on any other day; and that is the work of God. God rested on the seventh day, but he rested from creation; his higher works of judgment and mercy and compassion and love still went on and so did those of Jesus. Jesus teaches that human need must always be helped, and that there is no greater task than to relieve someone's pain and distress. Other works may be laid aside, but the work of compassion never. God calls us all to be compassionate. Just remember we stand tallest when we stoop to help others.

PRAYER

We beg you, Lord, to help and defend us. Deliver the oppressed. Pity the insignificant. Raise the fallen. Show yourself to the needy. Heal the sick. Bring back those of your people who have gone astray. Feed the hungry. Lift up the weak. Take off the prisoners' chains. May every nation comes to know that you alone are God, that Jesus is your Child, that we are your people, the sheep that you pasture. Amen

Commentary: The Romans allowed Jews a good deal of self-government, but they didn't have the right to carry out the death penalty. The ***ius gladii***, as it was called, the right of the sword which belonged only to the Romans. Forty years before the destruction of the Temple, judgment in matters of life and death was taken away from Israel. In some isolated cases the Jews would take the law into their own hand and execute someone (St. Stephen), but legally they had no right to inflict the death penalty on anyone. This is why they had to bring Jesus to Pilate before he could be crucified. If the Jews had themselves been able to carry out the death penalty, it would have been by stoning. The Law lays it down, and he who blasphemes the name of the Lord, shall be put to death, all the congregation shall stone him" (Leviticus 24: 16) In such a case the witnesses whose word proved the crime had to be the first to fling the stones.

They accused Jesus of claiming to be a king, although they knew that their accusation was a lie. Hatred is a terrible thing, and does

WE STAND TALLEST WHEN WE STOOP TO HELP OTHERS.

King's Game – On the surface of the Lithostrotos, various games are engraved in the pavement, which the Roman soldiers played to pass the time. One of the games, which, was very popular in the Roman army is the "Game of the King." It was in this area that Jesus was scourged.

not hesitate to twist the truth. When the Romans had first come into Palestine, they had taken a census in order to arrange the normal taxation to which people were liable. And there had been the most bloody rebellion, because the Jews insisted that God alone was their king, and to him alone they would pay tribute. When the Jewish leaders said: "We have no king but Caesar," it was the most astonishing bold face lie in history. I would think that this statement probably took Pilate's breath away and eventually took Jesus breath away.

John 19:1-17 Pilate's next move was to take Jesus and have him scourged. The soldiers then wove a crown of thorns and fixed it on his head, throwing around his shoulders a cloak of royal purple. Repeatedly they came up to him and said, "All hail, king of the Jews!" slapping his face as they did so.

Pilate went a second time and said to the crowd: "Observe what I do, I am going to bring him out to you to make you realize that I find no case against him." When Jesus came out wearing the crown of thorns and the purple cloak, Pilate said to them, "Look at this man!" As soon as the chief priest and temple guards saw him they shouted, "Crucify him! Crucify him!" Pilate said, "Take

Pilate presents Jesus to the people. Behold the man!

him and crucify him yourselves; I find no case against him." We have our law, the Jews responded, and according to that law he must die because he made himself God's Son. When Pilate heard this kind of talk, he was more afraid than ever. Going back into the praetorium, he said to Jesus, " Where do you come from?" Jesus would not give him any answer. "Do you refuse to speak to me?" Pilate asked him. "Do you not know that I have the power to release you and the power to crucify you?" Jesus answered: "You would have no power over me whatever unless it were given you from above. That is why he who handed me over to you is guilty of the greater sin."

After this, Pilate was eager to release him, but the Jews shouted, "If you free this man you are no Friend of Caesar. Anyone who makes himself a king becomes Caesar's rival." Pilate heard what they were saying, then brought Jesus outside and took a seat on a judge's bench at the place called the Stone Pavement – Gabbatha in Hebrew. (It was the Preparation day for Passover, and the hour was about noon.) He said to the Jews, "Look at your king!" At this they shouted, "Away with Him! Away with him! Crucify him! "What!" Pilate exclaimed. "Shall I crucify your king?" The chief priests replied, "We have no king but Caesar." In the end Pilate handed Jesus over to be crucified. Jesus was led away, and carries the cross by himself, went out to what is called the Place of the Skull – Golgotha in Hebrew.

REFLECTION

The carrying of the cross to Calvary has significant symbolism and I will try to explain several points which to discuss or reflect upon. Tradition has it that Jesus fell three times on the way to Calvary, but this cannot be proven and is part of holy tradition. The point

I would like to make is that tradition says He fell three times, and I believe that when He fell he must have fallen forward each time, so that when He got up he was that much closer to His objective, which was His crucifixion. Likewise, in our ordinary life we will fall too, but we pray that we fall forward and not backward, so when we get back up we too will be much closer to our own objective.

On the way to Calvary, Simon of Cyrene was forced into helping Jesus carrying the cross. We don't know that much about Simon of Cyrene, other than the fact that he came from Libya (North Africa) to celebrate Passover. Palestine was an occupied country, and all that a Roman officer had to do was to tap a Jew on the shoulder with the flat of his spear, and the man had to carry out any task, however menial and distasteful, that was laid upon him. Perhaps he was less than willing to help Jesus carry the cross that afternoon. Be that as it may, he touched a cross which was to be sought and venerated throughout the world, by generations yet unborn. More importantly, he participated in and, yes, even contributed to salvation history. His name is forever bound up with the most important event in human history. Simon was an average man, and when his average effort was made with Christ and for Christ, it became inextricably linked to eternity. There was nothing more written about this man, but the important thing is that he helped Jesus carry his cross. I personally believe that this 15-minute encounter that Simon of Cyrene had with Jesus, had to have a positive effect upon him. The important message here is that we all have to help other people carry their crosses very much like Simon of Cyrene did. First we have to identify these crosses, and determine which crosses come from our neighbors and friends, and which crosses come from God, and which crosses come from within our own self.

PRAYER

Lord, send your abundant blessing upon your people who devoutly recall the death of your Son in the sure hope of the resurrection. Grant us pardon; bring us comfort. May our faith grow stronger and our eternal salvation be assured. We ask this in your son's name Our Lord Jesus Christ. Amen.

JESUS LAYS DOWN HIS LIFE-GOOD SHEPHERD

John 10: 17-18 I am the good shepherd: the good shepherd lays down his life for the sheep. The Father loves me for this: that I lay down my life to take it up again. No one takes it from me; I lay it down freely. I have power to lay it down, and I have power to take it up again. This command I received from my Father.

Let us pray: Oh, Jesus, let me never forget Your love for me and the reparation You offered the Father for my sake. Let my soul magnify the Lord by humility of heart, purity of mind, and a gentle spirit. Lord Jesus you embraced your cross, but we so frequently shy away from the crosses You hold out to us. You have shown us that suffering without love is demeaning. But suffering embraced with love can become saving sacrifice. By your wounds we are healed, and in union with you, by our wounds, we can heal others. Fill our hearts with that selfless love by which you became our Savior. Grant this, Jesus Our Saving Lord. Amen.

HISTORY OF THE STATIONS OF THE CROSS

When Jesus died on the Cross, Joseph of Arimathea asked Pilate for the body and laid it in a new tomb (Jn 19 38-42). This was the typical Jewish tomb of the time, cut into the rock in the side of a

Jesus falls under the weight of the cross.

hill. It hadn't been used before, and, after the first Easter, the tomb was almost certainly not used again. It may have been the site of Christians commemoration, but by the early fourth century it was almost completely lost, with all the wars and invasions that went on in Jerusalem. It wasn't until Helena, the mother of the first Christian Roman Emperor started out looking for the Holy Sepulchre. She was told in a dream that the Tomb was completely covered under accumulated earth and that it had a shrine of Aphrodite built over it. Helena cleared away the pagan sanctuary and rocky hill as well, leaving the little cave-tomb and shell of rock around it, still attached to the bedrock. In the year 325 AD Helena built a church around the whole thing. People started visiting the Holy Sepulchre as a pious act, and in the Middle ages, priests started assigning trips to the Sepulchre as a penance for certain serious sins. Penitents would usually be shown the places in Jerusalem where, according to tradition recollection, certain key episodes of the Passion took place, and their trip culminated at the Sepulchre itself, from which Christ rose from the dead. Those who could make the trip to Jerusalem and back, under the prescribed conditions, received a plenary indulgence.

It's important to be clear on what an indulgence is, because those who don't understand it use the term so often in a disapproving way. An indulgence is remission of temporal punishment due to sin, provided that the sin has already been forgiven. That is sin, even after forgiveness though the sacrament of Reconciliation, merits punishment on Earth or in Purgatory. Temporal punishment, punishment that lasts only a time, is one of the ways that the sinner makes his adjustment to God. The Church has the power to remit this punishment with an indulgence, provided, again, that the person is in the state of grace, has the intention of gaining the indulgence, and performs the required acts. Traveling to Jerusalem has always been dangerous, not to mention expensive. A man would have to leave his work and family for as long as two years to make the trip, and his dependents would never know whether he'd make it back. Women with children, of course, couldn't make it at all. Well, this didn't make sense to a lot of Christians. It didn't seem fair to grant indulgences only to those rich enough or strong enough and lucky enough to make the trip halfway around the known world. What about those too ill, too weak, too tied to their fields and flocks? Why couldn't they get a plenary indulgence, too, if they fulfilled all of the conditions but didn't have the physical ability to travel?

During the Turkish occupation of the Holy Land in the late Middle Ages, pilgrims were prevented from visiting these sacred sites. The custom arose of making replicas of these holy places where faithful pilgrims might come to pray. One of the most popular of these devotions was the "Stations or Way of the Cross" which were imitations of the stopping places of prayer on the Via Dolorsa in Jerusalem. By the late sixteenth century a visual representation of the fourteen stations, as we know them today, was placed in almost all Catholic churches.

The Stations are:

I   *Jesus is condemned to death.* O Jesus! So meek and uncomplaining, teach me resignation in trials.

II   *Jesus takes up the Cross.* My Jesus, this cross should be mine, not Yours; my sins crucified You.

III   *Jesus falls under the Cross.* O Jesus! By this first fall, never let me fall into mortal sin.

IV   *Jesus meets his mother.* O Jesus! May no human tie, however dear, keep me from following the road of the Cross.

V   *Simon the Cyrenian is forced to carry the Cross.* Simon unwillingly assisted you; may I with patience suffer all for You.

VI   *Veronica wipes the sweat from Jesus' face.* O Jesus! You did imprint your sacred features upon Veronica's veil; stamp them also indelibly upon my heart.

Way of the Cross – Via Dolorosa composes the fourteen Stations of the Cross. Nine of these Stations are found in the Gospel, and five in tradition. The Stations are found within churches and chapels, as well as along the city streets, from the Lithostrotos to Golgotha.

VII   ***Jesus falls for the second time.*** By your second fall, preserve me, dear Lord, from relapse into sin.

VIII   ***Jesus consoles the women of Jerusalem.*** My greatest consolation would be to hear You say: "many sins are forgiven you, because you have loved much."

IX   ***Jesus falls for the third time.*** O Jesus! When weary upon life's long journey, be my strength and my perseverance.

X   ***Jesus is stripped of his garments.*** My soul has been robbed of its robe of innocence; clothe me dear Jesus with the garb of penance and contrition.

XI   ***Jesus is nailed to the Cross.*** You did forgive Your enemies; my God, teach me to forgive injuries and forget them.

XII   ***Jesus dies on the Cross.*** You are dying, my Jesus, but Your Sacred Heart still throbs with love for your sinful children.

XIII   ***Jesus is taken down from the Cross.*** Receive me into Your arms, O Sorrowful Mother; and obtain for me perfect contrition for my sins.

XIV   ***Jesus is laid in the Tomb.*** When I receive You into my heart in Holy Communion, O Jesus, make it a fit abiding place for Your adorable body.

DAMASCUS

Read near the Damascus Gate (Conversion of St. Paul)

Acts 9: 1-18 But Saul, still breathing out threat and murder to the disciples of the Lord, went to the high priest and asked him for letters of credit to Damascus, to the synagogues there, so that if he found any Christians, both men and women, he might bring them bound to Jerusalem. As he journeyed he came near Damascus. Suddenly a light from heaven flashed round about him. He fell on the ground and he heard a voice saying to him, "Saul, Saul, why do you persecute me?" He said, "Who, are you sir?" He said, "I am Jesus whom you are persecuting. But rise; go into the city, and you will be told what to do." His fellow-travelers stood speechless in amazement, because they heard the voice but saw no one. So Saul rose from the ground but when his eyes were opened he saw nothing. So they took him by the hand and led him into Damascus. And for three days he could not see, nor did he eat or drink anything. There was a disciple in Damascus called Ananias, and the Lord said to him in a vision, "Ananias." He said, "Here I am Lord." The Lord said to him, "Get up and go to the street called "Straight"; inquire in Judas's house for a man called Saul, a man from Tarsus. He is praying, and he has seen a man called Ananias coming and putting his hands on him so that he may get back his sight." Ananias answered, "Lord, I have heard from many about this man. They have told me all the hurt he has done to the saints at Jerusalem. They have told me too how he has authority from the chief priest to bind all who call upon your name." The Lord said to him, "Go, for he is a chosen instrument for my work. He is chosen to carry my name before peoples and kings and before the sons of Israel. I will tell him all he must suffer for my name's sake." So Ananias went away and came to the house. He put his hands on him and said, "Brother Saul, the Lord

Damascus Gate – The road to Damascus used to start here.

Jesus who appeared to you in the way on which you were going has sent me that you may get your sight back and so that you may be filled with the Holy Spirit." Thereupon things like scales fell from his eyes and he got his sight back again. He rose and was baptized, and he took food and his strength increased.

REFLECTION

Here we have the most famous conversion in history. Damascus is about 140 miles from Jerusalem and this journey would normally take about a week. We may want to enter Paul's mind and ask ourselves if this was a sudden conversion or a sudden surrender. Paul's only companions on the way to Damascus were the officers of the Sanhedrin, a kind of police force, and because he was a Pharisee, he could have nothing to do with them; so he probably walked alone. Just at that moment there came such a lightning storm and out of the storm Christ spoke to Paul. In that moment the long battle was over in an instant, and Paul surrendered to Christ. Paul continued his journey to Damascus a changed man. He had intended to enter Damascus with an avenging fury, but was led by the hand, blind and helpless.

Interesting enough Paul was doing what he liked, what he thought was best and what his will dictated. From this moment on, he would be told what to do. A Christian is any person who has ceased to do what they want to do, and who has begun to do what Christ wants them to do. How often we have to be knocked down and blinded, before we actually can see the light. Let us all pray for spiritual sight and for those who hate and persecute in the name of religious righteousness.

God our Father, you taught the Gospel to all the world through the preaching of Paul your apostle. May we who celebrate his conversion to the faith follow him in bearing witness to your truth. Bring new life to Jew and Gentile, man and woman, slave and free. Speak the word of life and love to all who dwell apart from you and are hostile to one another. We ask this through our Lord Jesus Christ, your Son, who lives and reigns with you and the Holy Spirit, one God, forever and ever. Amen

CHAPTER 4
(Upper Room, Caiaphas's House), Peter's Denial)
Washing of the Feet

Washing of the Feet
Mark 14: 12-17 (Jewish Passover Preparation)
John 13: 1-15

Priestly Prayer- Room of Last Supper
John 17: 20-26

1st Appearance to the Disciples
John 20: 19-28
John 17: 9-19

David's Tomb
Acts 2: 29-33

Caiaphas's High Priest House
Mark 14: 53-66
Psalm 88

Peter Is Arrested
Act 12: 1-11

Peter's Denial
Luke 22: 54-62
Luke 22: 31-34

UPPER ROOM COMMENTARY

The "upper room" was a second story room of a Palestinian house, often used for guests. It was in such a room that Jesus celebrated the Last Supper with his disciples. A fifth-century tradition locates this upper room on Mount Zion, the western hill of Jerusalem. The upper room, sometimes called the Cenacle ("supper room"), is today an empty room, with a few indications of its former use as both a Crusader church and an Islamic mosque. Nearby is the Franciscan Church of the Cenacle where the Eucharist is celebrated.

Preparations for the Last Supper were made on the first day of the Feast of Unleavened Bread. On this day the lambs were slaughtered in the temple and brought to each home for the Passover meal that evening (verse 12). In the gospels of Matthew, Mark, and Luke, the Last Supper is clearly a Passover meal, also called the Seder. Jesus, whose faith was firmly rooted in the religious traditions of his people, came to the city of pilgrimage at the time of its greatest feast.

The owner of the upper room is not known, but this is not surprising in a culture that placed such emphasis on hospitality and where especially at Passover all families open their doors to pilgrims and strangers. These festive meals at the time of Jesus were eaten while reclining on cushions. The elaborate rituals of the meal are not detailed in the gospels, neither is the recounting of the story of Exodus. Only the parts of the Seder meal given radically new significance by Jesus are highlighted. The food of the Passover, the unleavened bread, is identified as the body of Jesus . The ritual cup of wine is identified as the blood of Jesus, the blood of the covenant by which we enter a committed partnership with God.

Those of us who return in mind and heart to the upper room week after week, to do again what Jesus did there, share in the Paschal (Passover) mystery which joins us in the new covenant.

Tradition also associates this upper room with the appearance of the risen Jesus to his disciples (John 20: 19-29) and the descent of the Holy Spirit at Pentecost (Acts 2). Though this room is empty today, the events that took place in this upper room continue to live at the heart of the Christian faith. What happened here is now renewed over and over again across the world as the crucified and risen Lord gathers us as his people in the Holy Spirit.

REFLECTIONS

In this room, the greatest promises that ears have ever heard were made – and kept. Here Jesus spoke his last words. Here he promised that is we abide in him, we would bear much fruit. And then he fulfilled the promise by giving us the means to abide in him: "This is my body; this is my blood."

The room is empty now, but because of the promises made and kept here, are heart, lives and spirits are still full. We are living answers to Jesus' prayer. Our sins are forgiven, the Holy Spirit is with us, and we are strengthened by the Body and Blood of Jesus.

In this room he promised that although he was leaving us, he would not leave us orphans. "And I will pray to the Father, and he will give you another Counselor, to be with you forever, even the Spirit of truth, whom the world cannot receive, because it neither sees him nor knows him" (John 14:16-17). That promise he fulfilled in this room: "And there appeared to them, tongues as of fire….and they were all filled with the Holy Spirit" (Acts 2:3-4).

Here he promised: "Peace I leave with you." On the third day he returned to fulfill it: "Peace I leave with you. As the Father has sent me even so, I sent you….If you forgive the sins of any, they are forgiven; if you retain the sins of any, they are retained" (John 20:21,23).

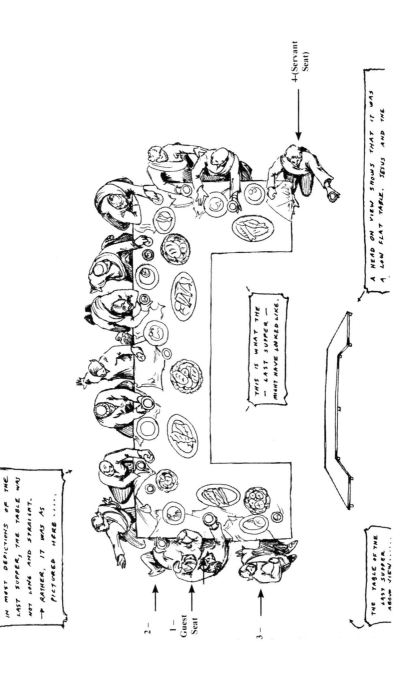

CONTRARY TO WHAT IS SEEN IN MOST DEPICTIONS OF THE LAST SUPPER, THE TABLE WAS NOT LONG AND STRAIGHT.
→ RATHER, IT WAS AS PICTURED HERE . . . . .

THIS IS WHAT THE — LAST SUPPER — MIGHT HAVE LOOKED LIKE.

A HEAD ON VIEW SHOWS THAT IT WAS A LOW FLAT TABLE. JESUS AND THE

THE TABLE OF THE LAST SUPPER. ABOVE VIEW . . . .

4 - (Servant Seat)

2 -

1 - Guest Seat

3 -

Here, Jesus prayed for us. "I do not pray for these only, but also for those who believe in me through their word" (John 17:2). That is ourselves! Jesus knew that you were going to be here in this room some 2000 years later.

PRAYER

Almighty God, you revealed yourself to your people as Yahweh: I am who am present to you. We rejoice in this hallowed room that you are present to us in your Son, Jesus. We praise you that on this spot he left us his presence in his Body and Blood. We praise you that he has fulfilled the promises made here; the Holy Spirit abides in us. May we never think we are alone again. We ask this in Jesus' name. Amen.

THE BETRAYER

Matt. 26: 24-26 When it was evening, he came with the Twelve. And as they reclined at table and were eating, Jesus said, "Amen, I say to you, one of you will betray me, one who is eating with me." They began to be distressed and to say to him, one by one, "Surely it is not I?" He said to them, "One of the Twelve, the one who dips with me into the dish. For the Son of Man indeed goes, as it is written of him, but woe to that man by whom the Son of Man is betrayed. It would be better for that man if he had never been born."

LAST SUPPER

Luke 22: 15-20 While they were eating, he took bread, said the blessing, broke it, and gave it to them, and said, "Take it; this is my body." Then he took a cup, gave thanks, and gave it to them, and they all drank from it. He said to them, "This is my blood of the covenant, which will be shed for many. Amen, I say to you, I shall not drink again the fruit of the vine until the day when I drink it new in the kingdom of God." Then, after singing a hymn, they went out to the Mount of Olives.

JEWISH PASSOVER PREPARATION

Mark 14: 12-17 On the first day of the Feast of Unleavened Bread, when they sacrificed the Passover lamb, his disciples said to him, "Where do you want us to go and prepare for you to eat the Passover?" He sent two of his disciple and said to them, "Go into the city and a man will meet you, carrying a jar of water. Follow him. Wherever he enters, say to the master of the house, "The Teacher says, where is my guest room where I may eat the Passover with my disciples?" Then he will show you a large upper room furnished and ready. Make the preparations for us there." The disciples then went off, entered the city, and found it just as he had told them, and they prepared the Passover.

REFLECTION

Jesus sent them into Jerusalem with instructions to look for a man carrying an earthen pitcher of water. To carry a water pot was a woman's duty. It was a thing that no man ever did except the Essenes (Essenes were the Orthodox Jews who work just like the woman. Josephus describes the three sects or schools into which the Jews were divided Pharisees, Sadducees, and the Essenes.) This was one reason why we believe that the Last Supper was celebrated in the Essene section of the Old City. The upper room had many uses. It was a storeroom, it was a place for quiet and meditation, it was a guest-room for visitors. But in particular it was the place where a Rabbi taught his chosen band of intimate disciples. What were the preparations that a Jew made for the Passover? Certain things were necessary and these were the things the disciples would have to get ready. There was the **lamb**, to remind them of how their houses had been protected by the badge of blood when the angel of death passed through Egypt. There was the **unleavened bread** to remind them of the bread they had eaten in haste when they escaped from slavery. There was a **bowl of salt water,** to remind them of the tears they had shed in Egypt and of the waters of the Red Sea through which they had miraculously

Jesus washes the feet of Peter.

passed to safety. There was a collection of **bitter herbs** – horse radish, chicory, lettuce, and endive to remind them of the bitterness of slavery in Egypt. There was a **paste called Charosheth**, a mixture of apples, dates, pomegranates and nuts to remind them of the clay of which they had made bricks in Egypt. There were **four cups of wine**. The cups contained a little more than half a pint of wine. The four cups, which were drunk at different stages of the meal, were to remind them of the four promises in Exodus 6: 6, 7. Such were the preparations, which had to be made for the Passover.

DRAWING OF LAST SUPPER TABLE

Most people have a tendency to think that the Last Supper Table was rectangular in shape very similar to most of the pictures drawn by Michelangelo. The table itself was shaped like a square with one side open. It was low and the guests reclined on couches, resting on their left arms with their right arms free for eating. There were certain positions at the table, that are numbered and will try to explain the apostles who sat at these locations. The guest at the table always sat at the #1 position located on the drawing, which would have been Jesus. We look at the # 2 and #3 positions at the table and try to associate which apostle according to scripture sat next to the guest (Jesus). On the left side would have been John because remember he was leaning on Jesus chest. Jesus' heart went out to the other apostle who sat next to him and yet Jesus knew he would betray him. This apostle was Judas #3 (" He who dips with me into the dish" Mark 14: 20). On the far side of the table at the #4 position usually sat the servant, but in this particular case it was one of the apostles. This particular apostle (Peter) felt hurt sitting in the servant seat, because he felt more important and was very proud. Once Judas leaves the room this is what happens, which is so important to understand. Jesus gives us an example on how we should act as Christians. Jesus the guest gets up and walks over to the servants seat, and washes the feet of Peter. **The guest washes the feet of the servant!** This is the example Jesus give to each of us. Regardless of our position in society we all have to be of service to those less fortune than us.

Washing of the Feet

John 13: 1-15 Before the feast of Passover, Jesus knew that his hour had come to pass from this world to the Father. He loved his own in the world and he loved them to the end. The devil had already induced Judas, son of Simon the Iscariot, to hand him over. So, during supper, fully aware that the Father had put everything into his power and that he had come from God and was returning to God, he rose from supper and took off his outer garments. He took a towel and tied it around his waist. Then he poured water into a basin and began to wash the disciples' feet and dry them with the towel around his waist. He came to Simon Peter, who said to him, "Master, are you going to wash my feet?" Jesus answered and said to him, "What I am doing, you do not understand now, but you will understand later." Peter said to him, "You will never wash my feet." Jesus answered him, "Unless I wash your feet, you will have no inheritance with me." Simon Peter said to him, "Master, then not only my feet, but my hands and head as well." Jesus said to him, "Whoever has bathed has no need except to have his feet washed, for he is clean all over; so you are clean, but not all." For he knew who would betray him; for this reason, he said, "Not all of you are clean." So when he had washed their feet and put his garments back on and reclined at the table again, he said to them, "Do you realize, what I have done for you? You call me "teacher" and "master", and rightly so, for indeed I am. If I, therefore, the master and teacher, have washed your feet, you

Room of Last Supper – The "Upper Room" located above the Tomb of David on Mount Zion, is believed to be the Cenacle in which Jesus ate the Passover with his disciples and celebrated the first Eucharist. Now as they were eating, Jesus took bread, and blessed, and broke it, and gave it to the disciples and said, "Take, eat; this is my body." Matthew 26: 26

ought to wash one another's feet. I have given you a model to follow, so that as I have done for you, you should also do."

REFLECTION

Few incidents in the New Testament reveal the character of Jesus and so perfectly show his love for his disciples as this reading. His hour of humiliation was near, but he also knew that his hour of glory was also near. At this particular moment Jesus shows us his humility and his love. Love is always like that. For example when someone becomes ill, the person who loves him will perform the most menial services and delight to do them, because love is like that. Sometimes we feel that we are too distinguished to do the humble things, too important to do

Jesus shows Thomas His wounds.

some menial task. Jesus was not like this, and we should not be either. He knew that he was Lord of all, and yet washed his disciples' feet. St. Francis was known to say: "the nearer we are to suffering humanity, the nearer we are to God." Just remember there is only one kind of greatness, and that greatness has to do with service to others. The world is full of people who are standing on their dignity when they ought to be kneeling at the feet of their sisters and brothers.

PRAYER

Jesus, come, my feet are dirty. You have become a servant for my sake, so fill your basin with water; come, wash my feet. I know that I am bold in saying this, but your own words have made me fearful; "If I do not wash your feet, you will have no companionship with me." Wash my feet, then, so that I may be your companion.

Thank you for calling me at this very moment in my life, and the opportunity to see where you were born, where you lived and where you died. Thank you and make me humble of heart. Amen

John 17: 20-26 "I do not pray for them alone. I pray also for those who will believe in me through their word, that all may be one as you, Father, are in me, and I in you; I pray that they may be (one) in us, that the world may believe that you sent me. I have given them the glory you gave me that they may be one, as we are one – I living in them, you living in me – that their unity may be complete. So shall the world know that you sent me. Father, all those you gave me I would have in my company where I am, to see this glory of mine which is your gift to me, because of the love you bore me before the world began. Father, the world has not known you, but I have known you; and these men have known that you sent me. To them I have revealed your name, and I will continue to reveal it so that your love for me may live in them, and I may live in them".

REFLECTION

Jesus said that He has given his disciples the glory, which his Father had given him. We must fully understand what that means. What was the glory of Jesus? There were several ways I think He talked of it. The Cross was his glory. Jesus did not speak of being crucified; he spoke of being glorified. Therefore, a Christian's glory will be the cross that he must bear. We should never think of our cross as a penalty, we must think of it as our glory. The harder the task a saint was given, the greater he considered its glory. The harder the task we give a student, or a craftsman, or a surgeon, the more we honor him or her. Jesus' perfect obedience to the will of God was His glory. We find our glory, not in doing as we like, but in doing as God wills. When we try to do as we like - as many of us have done- we find nothing but sorrow and disaster both for ourselves and for others. Again we find the real glory of life in doing God's will; the greater the obedience, the greater the glory. Jesus' glory lay in the fact that, from his life, men recognized his special relationship with God. They saw that no one could live as he did unless he was uniquely near to God. We should all strive to be God-like ourselves.

Jesus said that it was his will that his disciples should see his glory in the heavenly places. If we have to share Christ's Cross, we will then also share in his glory. If we have died with him, we shall also live with him. The joy we have now is only a faint foretaste of the joy, which is to come. It is Christ's promise that if we share his glory and his sufferings on earth, we shall share his glory and his triumph when life on this earth is ended. What greater promise could there be than that. In every ministry there is always a certain amount of suffering attached with it. From this prayer Jesus was to go straight out to the betrayal, the trial and the Cross. He was not to speak to his disciples again. It is a wonderful and precious thing to remember that before these terrible hours ahead of Him, His last words were not of despair but of glory.

Appearance to the Disciples

John 20: 19-28 On the evening of that first day of the week, even though the disciples had locked the doors of the place where they were for fear of the Jews, Jesus came and stood before them. " Peace

be with you," he said. When he had said this, he showed them his hands and his side. At the sight of the Lord the disciples rejoiced. " Peace be with you," he said again. " As the Father has sent me, so I send you." Then he breathed on them and said: "Receive the Holy Spirit. If you forgive men's sins, they are forgiven them; if you hold them bound, they are held bound."

Appearance to Thomas – It happened that one of the Twelve, Thomas (the name means "Twin") was absent when Jesus came. The other disciples kept telling him: "We have seen the Lord!" His answer was, "I will never believe it without probing the nail prints in his hands, without putting my finger in the nail marks and my hand into his side." A week later, the disciples were once more in the room, and this time Thomas was with them. " Peace be with you," he said; then, to Thomas: "Take your finger and examine my hands. Put your hand into my side. Do not persist in your unbelief, but believe!" Thomas said in response, "My Lord and my God!"

REFLECTION

It is most likely that the disciples continued to meet in this upper room where the Last Supper had been held. Jesus was suddenly in their midst and greeted them with "Peace be with you", which means may God give you every good thing, and may you be saved from trouble." Jesus gave his disciple a message, which was to be carried to all people, because he was going back to his Father. This sending out of man was parallel to the sending out of Christ by God. In this room Jesus made us all the messengers, and instruments of his word. It is our responsibility to carry on this message Jesus gave us.

Thomas never lacked courage and there can never be any doubt that he loved Jesus. He was so broken-hearted that he could not meet the other apostles, and wished to be alone in his grief. He sought loneliness rather than togetherness with his fellow apostles and as a result of this he missed the first coming of Jesus. We too can miss a lot in our life, if we let grief control us. Many times when sorrow and sadness strikes our life we have a tendency to shut other people out. This is the exact time when we do need other people in our life to help us through our difficult times. Thomas had several good virtues, as he refused to understand what he didn't understand or to believe, and what he did not believe. Thomas doubted in order to be sure, and when he was, he totally surrendered to God. We too, need to surrender to God, and what better place to do this than in the room of the Last Supper.

PRAYER

Jesus, give us all an intellect, a great intellect, for this only, that we may understand You better; because the better I get to know You, the more ardently will we love You. Jesus, we ask You for a powerful intellect, that we may understand divine and lofty matters. Jesus, give us a keen intellect with which I will get to know Your Divine Essence and Your inner, Triune life. Amen

JESUS' PRAYER FOR HIS DISCIPLES

John 17: 9-19 I pray for them. I do not pray for the world but for the ones you have given me, because they are yours, and everything of mine is yours and everything of yours is mine, and I have been glorified in them. And now I will no longer be in the world, but they are in the world, while I am coming to you. Holy Father, keep them in your name that you have given me, so they may be one just as we are. When I was with them I protected them in your name that you gave me, and I guarded them, and none of them was lost except the son of destruction, in order that the scripture might be fulfilled. But now I am coming to you. I speak this in the world so that they may share my joy completely. I gave them your word, and the world hated them, because they do not belong to the world any more than I belong to the world. I do not ask that you take them out of the world, but that you keep them from the evil one. They do not belong to the world any more than I belong to the world. Consecrate them in the truth. Your word is truth. As you sent me into the world, so I sent them into the world. And I consecrate myself for them, so that they also may be consecrated in truth.

Reflection

This passage tells us something about the disciples of Jesus. The disciples are given to Jesus by God. What does that mean? It means that the Spirit of God moves our hearts to respond to the appeal of Jesus. Through the disciples, glory has come to Jesus. The patient whom he has cured brings honor to a doctor; the scholar whom he has taught brings honor to the teacher; the athlete whom he has trained brings honor to his trainer. The men whom Jesus has redeemed bring honor to him. The bad man made good is the honor of Jesus. What Jesus does for the world is to send out his disciples into it, in order to lead it back to God and to make it aware of God. He prays for his men in order that they may be such as to win the world for him. Actually Jesus offers his men two things.

He offered them his joy. All he was saying to them was designed to bring them joy. He also offered them warning. He told them that they were different from the world, and that they could not expect anything else but hatred from it. Their values and standards were different from the world's. He never prayed that they might find escape, but he prayed that they might find victory. Our faith was never meant to withdraw a man from life, but to equip him better for it. It does not offer us a life in which troubles are escaped and evaded, but a life in which troubles are faced and conquered. We must never desire to abandon the world, but always desire to win it. Jesus also prayed for the unity of his disciples. Where there are divisions, where there is exclusiveness, where there is competition between the Churches, the cause of Christianity is harmed and the prayer of Jesus is frustrated. We must always remember that God has chosen us out, and dedicated us for his special service. That special service is that we should love and obey Him and should bring others to do the same. And God has not left us to carry out that great task with our own strength, but out of his grace He fits us for our task, if we place our lives in his hands.

Commentary On Confessions

The above reading is why we have confession. You may ask yourself why should I confess my sins to a Priest? He's only another human being and it is true, but he is a human being endowed by God to forgive sin in the name of God. The telling of our sins is not as farfetched as some of us might imagine. In Old Testament times before the coming of Christ, sacrifices of lambs, goats, and doves, etc. were offered by the priest for the people in the Temple of Jerusalem in atonement and for the forgiveness of their sins. The only way the specific sacrifice was determined was that the individual had to tell the priest what sin it was. Here immediately we see the pre-figuration of the Sacrament of Confession – the great gifts that would be bestowed on us by Jesus Christ. Jesus says to His Priests, "Whose sins you forgive are forgiven them, and whose sins you retain are retained." Now how would a Priest know whether to forgive your sins or to

Original Stairs to Caiaphas House - It is most probable that Jesus walked on these very stones leading to the High Priest House. Most of the buildings in Jerusalem have been destroyed numerous times, but oddly enough the original stairs still exist. These are the original stairs leading to Caiaphas House.

delay forgiveness unless you told him in his ear? Let me remind you of the story about the two blind men. In the first instance, the blind man approached Jesus. Jesus asked, "What do you want me to do for you?" The blind man replied to him, "Master, I want to see". Immediately he received his sight (Mark 10: 51-52). In the second instance a blind man makes the same request as the first that he may see, but Jesus acts very differently. First he stoops to the ground, takes some clay and mixes it with his spittle, smears it on the man's eyes, tells him to go and wash his eyes in the pool of Siloam, to go show himself to the priest and then he will be cured (John 9:1). Had you been present for both curing, would you not ask, "What is all this ceremony about?" Jesus who cured the first blind man instantly, certainly could have done the same with the second blind man, but for His own reason He did not choose to do it that way. And so it is with confession. Who are we to tell God how He should do it?

DAVID'S TOMB

Acts 2: 29-33 "Brothers, I can speak confidently to you about our father David. He died and was buried, and his grave is in our midst to this day. He was a prophet and knew that God had sworn to him that one of his descendants would sit upon his throne. He said that he was not abandoned to the nether world, nor did his body undergo corruption, thus proclaiming before hand the resurrection of the Messiah. This is the Jesus God has raised up, and we are His witnesses. Exalted at God's right hand, he first received the promised Holy Spirit from the Father, and then poured this Spirit out on us. This what you now see and hear."

Reflection

In this reading the Acts is out to prove that the sufferings and death of Christ were the fulfillment of prophecy. To the Jew the idea of a crucified Messiah was incredible. Their law said, "A hanged man is accursed by God" (Deuteronomy 21: 23-24). To the orthodox Jew the Cross made it completely impossible that Jesus could be the Messiah. The disciples would tell them that if you would only read your scriptures rightly you would see that all was foretold. After the Cross they were bewildered, broken men, with their dream gone and their lives shattered. It was the resurrection, which changed all that and turned them from cowards into heroes. <u>A man would never die for a lie</u>. If the apostles did not believe in Jesus Resurrection, they would never have followed Jesus. Even today it is difficult for people to understand His death and resurrection unless it is clearly explained. Sometimes God writes straight with crooked lines. He knows what He is doing, but we may not.

Jesus before the Sanhedrin.

Mark 14: 53-65 They led Jesus away to the high priest, and all the chief priests and the elders and the scribes came together. Peter followed him at a distance into the high priest's courtyard and was seated with the guards, warming himself at the fire. The chief priests and the entire Sanhedrin kept trying to obtain testimony against Jesus in order to put him to death, but they found none. Many gave false witness against him, but their testimony did not agree. Some took the stand and testified falsely against him, alleging, "We heard him say, I will destroy this temple made with hands within three days I will build another not made with hands." Even so their testimony did not agree. The high priest rose before the assembly and questioned Jesus, saying, "Have you no answer?

What are these men testifying against you?" But he was silent and answered nothing. Again the high priest asked him and said, "Are you the Messiah, the son of the Blessed One?" Then Jesus answered, "I am; and you will see the Son of Man seated at the right hand of the Power and coming with the clouds of heaven." At that the high priest tore his garments and said, "What further need have we of witnesses? You have heard the blasphemy. What do you think?" They all condemned him as deserving to die. Some began to spit on him. They blindfolded him and struck him and said to him, "Prophesy!" And the guards greeted him with blows.

REFLECTION

The power of the Sanhedrin was limited because the Romans were the rulers of the country. I think that Mark describes this meeting of the Sanhedrin as being compared to our Grand Jury. Its function was not to condemn, but to prepare a charge, which the criminal could be tried before the Roman governor. The Sanhedrin was the supreme court of the Jews and was composed of roughly seventy-one members. The High Priest (Caiaphas) presided over the court. The court sat in a semi-circle in such a way that any member could see any other member. Facing it sat the students of the Rabbis. They were allowed to speak on behalf of the person on trial but not against him. The court could not meet at night, nor could it meet at any of the great feasts. When evidence was taken, witnesses were examined separately, and their evidence to be valid must agree in every detail. Each individual member of the Sanhedrin must give his verdict separately, beginning from the youngest and going on to the eldest. If the verdict was a verdict of death, a night must elapse before it was carried out, so that the court might have a chance to change its mind and its decision toward mercy. It can be seen that

Author standing on original stairs leading up to the High Priest Caiaphas's House. When Jesus was arrested in the Garden of Gethsemane he was led up these actual stairs. Pilgrims coming with me will get a chance to walk where Jesus walked on these exact steps.

on point after point the Sanhedrin broke its own rules. It was a meeting at night. There is no word of individually given verdicts. A night was not allowed to elapse before the penalty of death was inflicted. In their eagerness to eliminate Jesus, the Jewish authorities did not hesitate to break their own laws. The Sanhedrin could get plenty of evidence they did not want, for there were many people who could come forward and say: I was a leper and he cleansed me. I was blind and he made able to see. I was deaf and he made me able to hear. I was lame and he made able to walk. I was paralyzed and he gave me back my strength." Now at last the High Priest takes the whole matter into this own hands, and ask Jesus a leading question, which was completely forbidden. No man could be asked to condemn himself, but that was the very question Caiaphas asked. We see the courage of Jesus, as he knew that to make that answer was to die, and yet unhesitatingly he made it. If only we too had the courage to speak the truth in difficult times. Let us all pray that we receive the strength to speak the truth, when difficult times enter

Peter weeps bitterly after denying Jesus.

our lives. The real tragedy here is that Jesus came to offer mankind love, but was denied even bare justice, and humiliated by the cruel horse-play of the Sanhedrin guards. Let us all go down into the pit and see where they kept him after his indictment.

READ IN THE PIT AT CAIAPHAS HOUSE
Taken from the book *City of God* by Venerable Mary of Agreda

By the ill-treatment, which the Lord received in the presence of Caiaphas, the wrath of this high priest and of all his supporters ands ministers was much gratified, though not at all satiated. But as it was already past midnight, the whole council of these men resolved

Church of St. Peter in Gallicantu – This church is located over the
site of the house of High Priest Caiaphas. After being arrested in
Gethsemane he is taken to this place to be tried for the first time
and is denied by Peter three times before the cock crows, as was predicted.

to take good care, that the Savior be securely watched and confined
until the morning, lest He should escape while they were asleep.
For this purpose they ordered Him to be locked, bound as He was,
in one of the subterranean dungeons, a prison cell set apart for the
most audacious robbers and criminals of the state. Scarcely any light
penetrated into this prison to dispel its darkness. It was filled with
such uncleanness and stench, that it would have infected the whole
house, if it had not been so remote and so well enclosed; for it had
not been cleaned for many years, both because it was so deep down

ands because of the degradation of the criminals that were confined in it; for none thought it worth making it more habitable than for mere wild beast, unworthy of all human kindness.

Read in the Pit at Caiaphas House

This is a pit in the house of Caiaphas the high priest and is the place that Jesus was kept until Friday morning. Since most Jews knew the psalms by memory, psalm 88 is most likely the prayer Jesus prayed while in the pit.

Psalm 88 O Lord, my God, by day I cry out; at night I clamor in your presence . Let my prayer come before you; incline your ear to my call for help, for my soul is forfeited with troubles and my life draws near to the nether world. I am numbered with those who go down into the pit; I am a man without strength, my couch is among the dead, like the slain who lie in the grave, whom you remember no longer and who are cut off from your care. You have plunged me into the bottom of the pit, into the dark abyss. Upon me your wrath lies heavy, and with all your billows you overwhelm me. You have taken my friends away from me; you have made me an abomination to them; I am imprisoned, and I cannot escape. My eyes have grown dim through affliction; daily I call upon you, O Lord; to you I stretch out my hands. Will you work wonders for the dead? Will the shades arise to give you thanks? Do they declare your kindness in the grave, your faithfulness among those who have perished? Are your wonders made known in the darkness or your justice in the land of oblivion? But I, O Lord, cry out to you; with my morning prayer I wait upon you. Why, O Lord, do you reject me; why hide from me your face? I am afflicted and in agony from my youth, I am dazed with the burden of your dread. Your furies have swept over me; your

terrors have cut me off. They encompass me like water all the day;
on all sides they close in upon me. Companion and neighbor you
have taken away from me, my only friend is darkness.

PETER GETS ARRESTED & FREED

Act 12: 1-11 About that time King Herod moved against some of
the believers, and killed the apostle James (John's brother). When
Herod saw how much this pleased the Jewish leaders, he arrested
Peter during the Passover celebration and imprisoned him, placing
him under the guard of sixteen soldiers. Herod's intention was to
deliver Peter to the Jews for execution after the Passover. But earnest
prayer was going up to God from the Church for his safety all the
time he was in prison. The night before he was to be executed, he was
asleep, double-chained between two soldiers with others standing
guard before the prison gate, when suddenly there was a light in the
cell and an angel of the Lord stood beside Peter. The angel slapped
him on the side to awaken him and said, " Quick! Get up!" And the
chains fell off his wrists! Then the angel told him "Get dressed and
put on your shoes." And he did. " Now put on your coat and follow
me!" the angel ordered. So Peter left the cell, following the angel. But
all the time he thought it was a dream or vision and didn't believe it
was really happening. They passed the first ands second cell blocks
ands came to the iron gate to the street, and this opened to them of
its own accord! So they passed through and walked along together
for a block, and then the angel left him. Peter finally realized what
had happened! " It's the Lord has sent his angel and saved me from
Herod and from what the Jews were hoping to do to me.

REFLECTION

There are two important points to remember in this reading: You notice that the angel told Peter "get dressed and put your shoes on", which means that the ordinary things in life we can do, we are supposed to do. The impossible things in life (like the chains and locked doors) should be left to God. We sometimes get bogged down and discouraged in life, when faced with some impossible tasks. Leave the impossible things for God, and just do the ordinary things that we can do.

PETER IN GALLICANTU
ROOSTER CROWS ON PETER

Luke 22: 31-34 Simon, Simon! Remember that Satan has asked for you, to sift you like wheat. But I have prayed for you that your faith may never fail. You in turn must strengthen your brothers." "Lord," He said to him, " at your side I am prepared to face imprisonment and death itself." Jesus replied, "I tell you Peter, the cock will not crow today until you have three times denied that you know me."

Luke 22: 54-62 They led him away under arrest and brought him to the house of the high priest, while Peter followed at a distance. Later they lighted a fire in the middle of the courtyard and were sitting beside it, and Peter sat among them. A servant girl saw him sitting in the light of the fire. She gazed at him intently, then said, "This man was with him." He denied the fact, saying," Woman, I do not know him." A little while later someone else saw him and said, "You are one of them too." But Peter said, "No, sir, not I!" About an hour after that another spoke more insistently: "This man was certainly with him, for he is a Galilean." Peter responded, "My friend, I do not know what you are talking about." At the very moment he was saying this, a cock crowed. **The Lord turned around and looked at Peter, and Peter remembered the word that the Lord had spoken to him. "Before the cock crows today you will deny me three times." He went out and wept bitterly.**

Reflection

In all fairness it is to be noted that Peter was one of the two disciples (John 18: 15) who had the courage to follow Jesus into the courtyard of the High Priest's house. Peter fell victim to a temptation, which could only have come to a brave man. The man of courage always runs more risks than the man who seeks a safe haven. Jesus did not speak to Peter in anger but looked at him in sorrow. The penalty of sin is to face, not the anger of Jesus, but the heartbreak in his eyes.

Chapter 5
Bethlehem
Shepard's Field
Bethlehem

Announcement to the Shepherds
Luke 2: 8-20

Christmas Carols

Genealogy of Jesus
Matthew 1: 17

Shepherd and the lost sheep
Matthew 18: 12-14

Magi comes to Bethlehem
Matthew 2: 13-18

Flight to Egypt
Matthew 2: 13-15

St. Jerome's Cave

Shepherd Field – A Bedouin guarding his flock on the margins
of the Judean Desert, near "Shepherds' Field".

Luke 2: 8-20 There were shepherds in that district living outside and keeping the night watch over their sheep. Then an angel of the Lord stood before them and the glory of the Lord surrounded them, and they were extremely afraid. The angel said to them, "Fear not! For behold, I announce good news of great joy which will be for all the people. For today was born for you a Savior, who is Christ the Lord, in the city of David. And this will be a sign for you: You will find a baby wrapped in cloth and lying in a manger." And suddenly there was a multitude of the armies of heaven with the angel, praising God and saying: Glory to God in the highest and on earth peace to men of good will! When the angels departed from them into heaven, the shepherds said to one another, "Let us go, therefore, to Bethlehem and see this thing which has happened, which the Lord has made know to us!" They went hurrying along, and they found Mary and Joseph and the baby lying in a manger, seeing it, they made known the word, which has been spoken to them about this Child. And all who heard were amazed at what was said to them by the shepherds. But Mary kept all these words, considering them in her heart. The shepherds returned glorifying and praising God for everything, which they heard and saw.

REFLECTION

It was to the simple man (the Shepherd) that God's message first came to this world. The Shepherds were seen in the Temple both morning and evening as their unblemished lambs were being offered daily as a sacrifice to God. It is most likely that these Shepherds were in charge of the flocks from which the Temple offerings were chosen. It is a warm and lovely thought that the shepherd, who looked after the Temple lambs, were the first to see the Lamb of God who takes away the sin of the world. It is nice to know that we have a God who knows the life we live, because he too, lived it and claimed no special advantage over the common man.

PRAYER

Gracious Father Your word, spoken in love, created the human family and Your Son, conceived in love, restored it to Your friendship. Hear the prayers of all women who await the birth of their child. Calm their fears when they are anxious. Watch over and support these parents and bring their child into this world safely and in good health, so that as members of your family they may praise You and glorify You through your Son, our Lord Jesus Christ, now and forever. Amen

Songs to sing in Bethlehem and Shepherds field:

AWAY IN A MANAGER

Away in a manger, no crib for a bed,
The little Lord Jesus laid down His sweet head;
 The stars in the sky, look'd down where He lay,
The little Lord Jesus asleep on the hay.
The cattle are lowing, the poor baby wakes,
But little Lord Jesus, no crying He makes;
I love Thee, Lord Jesus! Look down from the sky,
And stay by my cradle till morning is nigh.
Be near me, Lord Jesus, I ask Thee to stay
Close by me forever and love me, I pray;
Bless all the dear children in Thy tender care,
And take us to heaven, to live with Thee, there.

LITTLE TOWN OF BETHLEHEM

O little town of Bethlehem how still we see thee lie!
Thy deep and dreamless sleep the silent stars go by;
Yet in thy dark streets shineth the everlasting Light;
The hopes and fears of all the years are met in thee
    tonight.
For Christ is born of Mary, And gathered all above,
O little town of Bethlehem, How still we see thee lie!
While mortals sleep, the angels keep, their watch of
    wond'ring love.
O morning stars, together Proclaim the holy birth,
And praises sing to God the King, And peace to men on
    earth.

O COME ALL YE FAITHFUL

O come, all ye faithful, joyful and triumphant,
O come ye, O come ye to Bethlehem.
Come and behold Him, born the King of Angels.
Refrain: O come let us adore Him, O come let us adore
   Him, O come let us adore Him, Christ the Lord.
Sing choirs of angels, sing in exultation Sing, all ye citizens
   of heaven above. Glory to God, in the highest.
Refrain

JOY TO THE WORLD

Joy to the world! The Lord is come:
Let earth receive her King;
Let every heart prepare Him room,
And heaven and nature sing, and heaven and nature sing,
   And heaven, and heaven and nature sing.
Joy to the world! The Savior reigns;
Let men their songs employ;
While fields and floods, rocks, hills and plains,
Repeat the sounding joy,
Repeat the sounding joy, Repeat, repeat the sounding joy.

SILENT NIGHT

Silent Night, Holy Night, All is calm, all is bright Round
   yon Virgin, Mother and Child
Holy Infant, so tender and mild
Sleep in heavenly peace, sleep in heavenly peace.
Silent Night, Holy Night, shepherds quake at the sight,

Glories stream from heaven afar, Heavenly host sing
   Alleluia!
Christ, the Savior is born,
Christ, the Savior is born.

ANGELS WE HAVE HEARD ON HIGH

Angels we have heard on high, Singing sweetly through the
   night,
And the mountains in reply, Echoing their brave delight.
Refrain:
Gloria in excelsis Deo
Shepherds, why this jubilee?
Why these songs of happy cheer?
What great brightness did you see?
What glad tiding did you hear?
Refrain:
Gloria in excesis Deo

O HOLY NIGHT

O holy night! The stars are brightly shining,
It is the night of the dear Savior's birth!
Long lay the world in sin and error pining,
Til He appeared and the soul felt its worth.
A thrill of hope the weary soul rejoices,
For yonder breaks a new and glorious morn!
Fall on your knees! O hear the angel voices!
O night divine! O night when Christ was born.
O night divine! O night, O night divine!

12 DAYS OF CHRISTMAS (EDUCATION)

There is one Christmas Carol that has always baffled me.

What in the world does leaping lords, French hens, swimming swans, and especially the partridge who won't come out of the pear tree have to do with Christmas? Today I found out, thanks to the Internet... this came from a friend.

From 1558 until 1829, Roman Catholics in England were not permitted to practice their faith openly. Someone during that era wrote this carol as a catechism song for young Catholics. It has the two levels of meaning: the surface meaning plus a hidden meaning known only to members of their church. Each element in the carol has a code word for a religious reality which the children could remember.

The partridge in a pear tree was Jesus Christ.

Two turtle doves were the Old and New Testaments.

Three French hens stood for faith, hope and love.

The four calling birds were the four gospels of Matthew, Mark, Luke & John.

The five golden rings recalled the Torah or Law, the first five books of the Old Testament

The six geese a-laying stood for the six days of creation.

Seven swans a-swimming represented the sevenfold gifts of the Holy Spirit: Prophesy, Serving, Teaching, Exhortation, Contribution, Leadership, and Mercy.

The eight maids a-milking were the eight beatitudes.

Nine ladies dancing were the nine fruits of the Holy Spirit: Love, Joy, Peace, Patience, Kindness, Goodness, Faithfulness, Gentleness, and Self Control.

The ten lords a-leaping were the ten commandments.

The eleven pipers piping stood for the eleven faithful disciples.

Star of Bethlehem – The famous silver star marks the site of the birth
of Jesus Christ in the Grotto. Upon it there is a Latin inscription
which says: "Here Jesus Christ was born of the Virgin Mary".

The twelve drummers drumming symbolized the twelve points of belief in the Apostles' Creed.

So there is your history for today. This knowledge was shared with me and I found it interesting and enlightening and now I know how that strange song became a Christmas Carol.

THE SHEPHERD AND THE LOST SHEEP

Matthew 18:12-14 "What do you think? If a man has a hundred sheep, and one of them wanders away, will he not leave the ninety-nine, and go out to the hills, ands will he not seek the wandering one? And if he finds it, this is the truth I tell you. He rejoices more over it than over the ninety-nine who never wandered away. So it is not the will of your Father that one of these little ones should perish."

Bethlehem – a little town of Arab Muslims and Christians
that stands on a rocky hill about 2,600 feet above sea level.
Notice the small door and entrance to the Church of the Nativity.
The small door was designed this way to prevent conquering
horseman from destroying the church on horseback. The low door
force each person who entered this holy precinct to bow to its sanctity.

The author standing next to the small doorway
entrance to the Church of the Nativity.

Reflection

In Judea it was tragically easy for sheep to go astray. The sheep and goats all recognize the tone of voice of the Shepherd, and would easily follow the Shepherd wherever he goes. There are no restraining walls or fences in the country, which would keep them from wandering. This short parable teaches us several things: **The love of God is an individual love.** Even though ninety-nine sheep were found, the Shepherd was not content until the last one was found. God is like that with us. He will not be happy until the last wanderer is gathered in. **The love of God is a patient love.** The sheep might be foolish, but the shepherd would still risk his life to save it. Men may be fools, but God loves even the foolish man who has no one to blame but himself for his sin and his sorrow. **The love of God is seeking love.** The shepherd was not content to wait for the sheep to come back, but he went out to search for it. God is not content to wait until men come home, He goes out to search for them no matter what it costs Him. God feels that we are all important in His eyes. **The love of God is a rejoicing love.** It is human never to forget a man's past and always to remember his sins against Him. God puts our sins behind His back, and when we return to Him, it is all joy. **The love of God is a protecting love.** It is the love, which seeks and saves. There can be a love, which ruins, there can be a love, which soften, but the love of God is a protecting love, which saves a man for the service of his fellow man. God will use you to touch other people, if you only let him. In the psalms it says that: The Lord is kind and merciful; slow to anger, and rich in compassion. We too should all strive to be kind and merciful, slow to anger and rich in compassion.

Birth of Jesus.

Matthew 1: 17
Thus the total number of generations from Abraham to David is Fourteen generations; from David to the Babylonian exile is Fourteen generations; from the Babylonian exile to the Messiah, Fourteen generations.

The Silver Star on the floor of the grotto has 14 points, which is symbolic of the 14 generations in the genealogy of Christ. The Silver Star goes back to the year 1717 with the Latin inscription over it, which says, "Here Jesus Christ was born of the Virgin Mary".

HISTORICAL

Censuses were taken every fourteen years with the double objective of assessing taxes and of discovering those who were liable for compulsory military service. The Jews were exempt from military service and therefore the censuses taken were merely for taxation purpose only. Men had to go to their own city or the headquarters of their own tribe. For Joseph it, meant going to Bethlehem.

I thought it quite interesting that "**there was no room in the inn**" was symbolic of what was to happen to Jesus. The only place where there was room for him was on a cross. He sought an entry to the over-crowded hearts of men; He could not find it; and still His search and His rejection goes on.

SPIRITUAL READING FOR THE CHURCH OF THE NATIVITY

REFLECTION

We look with wonder at the wisdom of God as the promised woman gives birth to the Promised Messiah in a cold cave! Deprived of all material things, the Splendor of Heaven entered the world in

Inside the Church of the Nativity – The original church was built by the Emperor Constantine in 326 AD and later restored by the Emperor Justinian in 529. It was later enhanced by the Crusaders. Joseph also went up from Galilee, from the city of Nazareth, to Judea, to the city of David, which is called Bethlehem, because he was of the house and lineage of David, to be enrolled with Mary, his betrothed, who was with child.

abject poverty. Jesus and Mary want us to know that their love for us is pure and devoid of any selfishness. The Mother of God says to all Mothers. "Let the dignity of your Motherhood rise above created things and the richness of your love cover your poverty". Can we ever imagine the ecstasy of Mary as her eyes met the eyes of God in her tiny infant? Can our hearts ever feel the agony as she saw His outstretched arms form a cross? Can we in our finest moments ever fathom such love and pain? Sweet mother, we want to take our place with the Shepherds to tell Jesus of our love and gratitude. We want to reach out to the men of all nations just as the Infant reaches out to the Wise Men of the East. We want to put aside our prejudice and bigotry and offer the gift of our love to all men. Obtain for us the grace to see Jesus in the lowly and offer Jesus to the forgotten.

Teach us how to be holy, so we may give the Father the glory and Jesus the pleasure of making sinners into saints.

MAGI

Matthew 2: 1-12 When Jesus was born in Bethlehem of Judea, in the days of King Herod, behold, magi from the east arrived in Jerusalem, saying, "Where is the newborn king of the Jews? We saw his star at its rising and have come to do him homage." When King Herod heard this, he was greatly troubled, and all Jerusalem with him. Assembling all the chief priests and the scribes of the people, he inquired of them where the Christ was to be born. They said to him, "In Bethlehem of Judea, for thus it has been written through the prophet: And you, Bethlehem, lands of Judah, are by no means least among the rulers of Judah; since from you shall come a ruler, who is the shepherd of my people Israel." Then Herod called the magi secretly and ascertained from them the time of the star's appearance. He sent them to Bethlehem and said, "Go and search diligently for the child. When you have found him, bring me word, that I may go and do him homage." After their audience with the kings they set out. And behold, the star that they had seen at its rising preceded them, until it came and stopped over the place where the child was. They were overjoyed at seeing the star, and on entering the house they saw the child with Mary his mother. They prostrated themselves and did him homage. Then they opened their treasures and offered him gifts of gold, frankincense, and myrrh. And having been warned in a dream not to return to Herod, they departed for their country by another way.

Reflection

From very early times men have seen a peculiar relationship in the gifts the wise men brought. They have seen in each gift something, which specially matched some characteristic of Jesus and his work. **Gold**, the king of metal is the gift fit for a king of men. **Frankincense** is the gift for a priest. It was in the Temple worship and at the Temple sacrifices that the sweet perfume of frankincense was used. The function of a priest is to open the way to God for men. **Myrrh** is the gift for one who is to die. Myrrh was used to embalm the bodies of the dead. Jesus came into the world to die. Gold for a king, frankincense for a priest, and myrrh for one who was to die. These were the gifts of the wise men, and even at the cradle of Christ, they foretold that he was to be the true King, the perfect High Priest, and in the end the supreme Savior of men.

Prayer

Lord, bless all who look upon this manger; may it remind us of the humble birth of Jesus, and raise our thoughts to him, who is God with us and Savior of all, and who lives and reigns for ever and ever. Amen

Commentary on Herod

Herod had one terrible flaw in his character. He was almost insanely suspicious. He had always been suspicious, and the older he became, the more suspicious he grew. He murdered his wife, and her mother, and several of his sons. Augustus, the Roman Emperor, had said bitterly, that it was safer to be Herod's pig than Herod's son. When Herod was seventy, and he knew he would die, he retired to Jericho, and gave orders that a collection of the most distinguished citizens of Jerusalem should be arrested on trumped-up charges and imprisoned. He ordered that the moment he died, they should all be killed. He said grimly that

Joseph & Mary fleeing to Egypt

he was well aware that no one would mourn for his death, and that he was determined that some tears should be shed when he died.

HOLY INNOCENTS

Matthew 2: 13-18 After the Magi had left, the angel of the Lord suddenly appeared in a dream to Joseph with the command: "Get up, take the child and his mother, and flee to Egypt, Stay there until I tell you otherwise. Herod is searching for the child to destroy him." Joseph got up and took the child and his mother

and left that night for Egypt. He stayed there until the death of Herod, to fulfill what the Lord had said through the prophet: "Out of Egypt I have called my son." Once Herod realized that the Magi had deceived him, he became furious. He ordered the massacre of all the boys two years old and under in Bethlehem, and its surrounding area making his calculations on the basis of the date he had learned from the astrologers. What was said through Jeremiah the prophet was then fulfilled: "A cry was heard at Ramah, sobbing and loud lamentation: Rachel bewailing her children; no comfort for her, since they are no more."

COMMENTARY

Actually, St. John the Baptist should have been killed along with the holy innocents. The home of John the Baptist was located in the area surrounding Bethlehem, and would have been included in the area which Herod's soldiers would have searched for him. Tradition has it that Elizabeth was warned by an angel to hide the child. When the soldiers came, they saw Elizabeth who was older in age and obviously too old to be a mother, and did not search their house thoroughly. Elizabeth hid John behind a well near her cottage. When visiting the Church of the Visitation look for the well which John was hidden behind?

REFLECTION

The ancient world had no doubt that God sent his messages to men in dreams. Throughout the centuries before Jesus came, whenever the Jews suffered tyranny or persecution they usually sought refuge in Egypt. Egypt was proverbially known as the land of sorcery, of witchcraft and of magic. The Talmud says, "Ten measures of sorcery descended into the world, and Egypt received nine, the rest of the world one." Many of the enemies of Jesus during his life declared that it was in Egypt that Jesus had learned magic and sorcery, which made him able to work miracles, and to deceive men.

INTERESTING LEGEND

Legend calls the penitent thief Dismas, and tells that he did not meet Jesus for the first time when they both hung on their crosses on Calvary. The story runs like this. When Joseph and Mary were on their way to Egypt, robbers overcame them. One of the robbers' chiefs wished to murder them at once and to steal their little store of goods. But something about the baby Jesus went straight to Dismas's heart, for Dismas was one of these robbers. He refused to allow any harm to come to Jesus or his parents. He looked at Jesus and said, "O most blessed of children, if ever there come a time for having mercy on me, then remember me, and forget not this hour." So, the legend says, Jesus and Dismas met again at Calvary, and Dismas on the cross found forgiveness and mercy for his soul.

BEDOUINS' AKA (SHEPHERDS)

The Bedouin have a custom, which goes back to the Biblical Times. If you are lucky enough to be invited to have tea with them in their tents they will serve you three cups of tea. The first two cups of tea are very bitter and the third cup of tea is sweet. This tradition goes back to the biblical time as they want you to experience the bitter things in life first, before you can enjoy the sweet things. How true this is in our own lives. Many of us have experienced the bitter things in life and are now looking forward to the sweets things. Maybe this trip to the Holy Land is the beginning of the sweet things to come? Oh Jesus, I never knew God until you showed me.

ST JEROME (SEPT 30)
(Read in the cave near his tomb-Bethlehem)

Saint Jerome who is called in Latin, **Hieronymus**, which means **holy name**-, was born in Dalmatia. He was baptized a Catholic when he was eighteen years old, after living as a hermit in Palestine, St. Jerome came to Rome. Much against his will, because of his great humility, he was ordained a priest. He was a great friend and ally of St. Damasis, the thirty-ninth Pope. St. Damasus commissioned Jerome to translate the whole Bible into Latin. It took St. Jerome 14 years to make his first version in Latin of the Holy Scripture, in what is known as the Vulgate. A few more years were required to make recommendations, and then in the beginning of the Fifth Century, Latin became the language of the Church in Jerome's style, the perpetual prayer of Catholics.

Saint Jerome had a great devotion and love for the Blessed Virgin Mary. He went to Bethlehem, lived near the crib where Our Lord was born. St. Jerome also had strong devotion to Guardian Angel. He was also known as a Doctor of the Church who assures us and the Church has completely confirmed this, that each one of us has a Guardian Angel for himself. It was also St. Jerome who beautifully let us know that St. Cleophas was the brother of St. Joseph. This explains why St. James, St. Simon, and St. Jude, the sons of St. Cleophas, and St. James the Greater and St. John, his grandsons, are referred to as the "brethren of Our Lord". In Hebrew and Aramaic there isn't another word to mean cousin so they use the word brethren. St. Jerome died in Bethlehem, and is one of the thirty-two Doctors of the Universal Church.

CHAPTER 6

**Ein Karem, John the Baptist House
Church of the Visitation- Ein Karem**

St. John the Baptist House
Luke 1: 5-26

Visitation of Mary to Elizabeth
Luke 1: 39-56

Magnificat
Matthew 7: 7-12 (The Answer to Prayer)

Road to Emmaus
Luke 24: 13-35

Inspirational Thoughts

Zechariah House

Luke 1: 5-26

 In the days of Herod, King of Judea, there was a priest named Zechariah of the priestly division of Abijah; his wife was from the daughters of Aaron, and her name was Elizabeth. Both were righteous in the eyes of God, observing all the commandments and ordinances of the Lord blamelessly. But they had no child, because Elizabeth was barren and both were advanced in years.

Once when he was serving as priest in his division's turn before God, according to the practice of the priestly service, he was chosen by lot to enter the sanctuary of the Lord to burn incense. Then, when the whole assembly of the people was praying outside at the hour of the incense offering, the angel of the Lord appeared to him, standing at the right of the altar of incense. Zechariah, was troubled by what he saw, and fear came upon him. But the angel said to him, "Do not be afraid, Zechariah, because your prayer has been heard. Your wife Elizabeth will bear a son, and you shall name him John. And you will have joy and gladness, and many will rejoice at his birth, for he will be great in the sight of the Lord. He will drink neither wine nor strong drink. He will be filled with the Holy Spirit even from his mother's womb, and he will turn many of the children of Israel to the Lord their God. He will go before him in the spirit and power Elijah to turn the hearts of father toward children and disobedience to the understanding of the righteous, to prepare a people fit for the Lord. Then Zechariah said to the angel, " How shall I know this? For I am an old man, and my wife is advanced in years." The angel said to him in reply, "I am Gabriel, who stands before God. I was sent to speak to you and to announce to you this good news. But now you will be speechless and unable to talk until the day these things take place, because you did not believe my words, which will be fulfilled at their proper time."

Meanwhile the people were waiting for Zechariah and were amazed that he stayed so long in the sanctuary. But when he came out, he was unable to speak to them, and they realized that he had seen a vision in the sanctuary. He was gesturing to them but remained mute. Then, when his days of ministry were completed, he went home.

After this time his wife Elizabeth conceived, and she went into seclusion for five months, saying, " So has the Lord done for me at a time when he has seen fit to take away my disgrace before others."

REFLECTION

It was in God's house that God's message came to Zechariah. We may often wish that a message from God would come to us. They do come, if you pray from your heart and then listen you will hear Him. Zechariah was in the Temple waiting on God. God's voice comes to those who listen for it-as Zechariah did in God's house. Sometimes waiting for God is like swimming in a lake, and you have to wait for the currents of life to move us.

CANTICLE OF ZECHARIAH

Blessed be the Lord, the God of Israel;
He has come to his people and set them free.
He has raised up for us a mighty savior,
Born of the house of his servant David.
Through his holy prophets he promised of old
That he would save us from our enemies,

From the hands of all who hate us.

He promised to show mercy to our fathers.

And to remember his holy covenant.

This was the oath he swore to our father Abraham:

To set us free from the hands of our enemies, free to
   worship

Without fear, holy and righteous in his sight all the days of
   our life.

You, my child, shall be called the prophet of the most High;

For you will go before the Lord to prepare his way, To give
   his people knowledge of salvation by the forgiveness
   of their sins. In the tender compassion of our God the
   dawn from on high shall break upon us, To shine on
   those who dwell in darkness and the shadow of death,
   And to guide our feet into the way of peace.

Glory to the Father, and to the Son, and to the Holy Spirit,

As it was in the beginning, is now, and will be for ever.

Amen

Luke 1: 39-56 Mary set out, proceeding in haste into the hill country to a town of Judah, where she entered Zechariah's house and greeted Elizabeth. When Elizabeth heard Mary's greeting, the baby stirred in her womb. Elizabeth was filled with the Holy Spirit, and cried out in a loud voice;" Blessed are you among women and blessed is the fruit of your womb. But who am I that the mother of my Lord should come to me? The moment your greeting sounded in my ears, the baby stirred in my womb for joy. Blessed is she who trusted that the Lord's words to her would be fulfilled." Mary said, "My being proclaims the greatness of the Lord, my spirit finds joy in God my savior, for he has looked upon his servant in her lowliness; all ages to come shall call me blessed. God who is

Church of the Visitation - and she exclaimed with a loud cry, "Blessed are you among women, and blessed is the fruit of your womb! The church of the Visitation, also known as the Church of the Magnificat, in Ein Karem commemorates the meeting of Mary with Elizabeth.

mighty has done great things for me, holy is his name; his mercy is from age to age on those who fear him. He has shown might with his arm; he has confused the proud in their inmost thoughts. He has deposed the mighty from their thrones and raised the lowly to high places. The hungry he has given every good thing, while the rich he has sent away empty. He has upheld Israel his servant, ever mindful of his mercy; even as he promised our fathers, promised Abraham and his descendants forever." Mary remained with Elizabeth about three months and then returned home.

REFLECTION

To Mary was granted the blessedness of being the mother of the Son of God. Well might her heart be filled with a wonder and tremendous joy at such a great privilege. If God chose her to take care of His own Son, how much more and even better can she take care of us. Mary's Son came into this world not to make life easy, but to make us all great. Mary did enjoy the greatest of joy of being Jesus' mother, but she also had the greatest of all tasks. Our Lady's responsibility is to bring all of us to her Son, and who knows more about the Son than the mother.

PRAYER

The Lord has bestowed the fruits of the earth for the benefits of all the world's people. May we share with all in need and so be good stewards of God's earth and its abundance. We remember the words Mary speaks in the gospel story of the visitation: "The hungry he has filled with good things." You shall eat and be filled and shall praise the name of the Lord, your God, because he has dealt wondrously with you. Thanks be to God. Amen

MAGNIFICAT

My soul magnifies the Lord, and my spirit rejoices in God my Savior; because He has regarded the lowliness of His handmaid; for behold, henceforth all generations shall call me blessed; because He who is mighty has done great things for me, and holy is His name; and His mercy is from generation to generation on those who fear Him. He has shown might with His arm, He has scattered the proud in the conceit of their heart. He has put down the mighty from their thrones, and has exalted the lowly. He has filled the hungry with

Mary visits Her Cousin Elizabeth

good things and the rich He has sent away empty. He has given help to Israel, his servant, mindful of His mercy even as He spoke to our fathers- to Abraham and to his posterity forever.

SPIRITUAL READING AT THE CHURCH OF VISITATION

What impulse of love made you hurry to visit your cousin Elizabeth, kind Mother? At a moment when you had every right to rest in the jubilant news that you would be the Mother of the Messiah you left the place of your exaltation. No doubt the advanced age of Elizabeth caused you concern. Your compassionate heart turned toward her.

Elizabeth, in her old age, needed the comfort of your youth. The child in your womb, conceived by the Holy Spirit, began His work of Redemption by sanctifying John. Your zeal to carry Jesus to others, no matter what the cost, embarrasses us and causes us to blush with shame. We neglect the aged because we are too busy. We permit the Generation Gap to widen because we do not possess the love to bridge the distance. We permit social injustice because we do not wish to be our brother's keeper. Holy Mary, bring Jesus to us through the merits of your visit to Elizabeth. Obtain for us the graces we need to magnify the Lord by our humility in dealing with our neighbor, our concern for the aged, our zeal for social justice and our courage when duty calls for sacrifice.

COMMENTARY

Ein Karm, which means "The Spring of the Vineyard" because of the abundance of springs to water the many vineyards and orchards nearby. (The short tunnel in the crypt is a cave at the farthest end, with a short first century stone vault and a longer Byzantine vault. It contains the well where, by tradition, our Lady met Elizabeth and also John was later hidden from Herod's soldiers. **Fresco** depicts Zechariah in the Temple offering incense. The second fresco depicts the Visitation. Elizabeth is bent over as Baby John leaps for joy. The third is a slaughter of the Holy Innocents.

THE ANSWER TO PRAYER

Matthew 7: 7-12 Ask and it will be given to you; seek and you will find; knock and the door will be opened to you. For everyone who asks, receives; and the one who seeks, find; and to the one who knocks, the door will be opened. Which one of you would hand

his son a stone when he asks for as loaf of bread, or a snake when he asks for a fish? If you then, who are wicked, know how to give good gifts to your children, how much more will your heavenly Father give good things to those who ask Him.

REFLECTION

Any person who prays usually wants to know to what kind of God, I am praying to. They want to know in what type of atmosphere will their prayers be heard. Are we praying to a God whose heart is so kind that He is more ready to give than we are to ask? The Jewish Rabbis said the loveliest things about prayer, "God is a near to his creatures as the ear to the mouth." Human beings can hardly hear two people talking at once, but God, if all the world calls out to Him at the same time, hears each and everyone of their cries. God the Father will never refuse the requests of his children, and will never mock our prayers. Very importantly God will always answer our prayers, but He will answer them **in His way**, and His way will be the way of perfect wisdom and of perfect love. Jesus is telling us to persist in our prayers, and clearly there lies the test of our sincerity. In this reading Jesus lays down the twin facts that God will always answer our prayer in his way, in wisdom and in love, and that we must bring to God an undiscouraged life of prayer, which test the rightness of the things we pay for, and which tests our own sincerity in asking for them.

EMMAUS

About seven miles from Jerusalem, toward the coast, is the small town of Emmaus or in Arabic called Qubeiba. This a quiet place with its splendid view of the country side toward the Mediterranean, and is an excellent place for prayer and reflection. Tradition holds that this is the spot where Jesus' two disciples recognized him in the breaking of the Bread on Easter Sunday. Tradition also holds that Cleophas one of the men who Jesus appears to is actually his uncle. Cleophas is St. Joseph's brother, which makes Jesus his Nephew.

Luke 24: 13-35 Two of them that same day were making their way to a village named Emmaus, seven miles distant from Jerusalem, discussing as they went all that had happened. In the course of their lively exchange, Jesus approached and began to walk along with them. However, they were restrained from recognizing Him. He said to them, "What are you discussing as you go your way?" They halted, in distress, and one of them, Cleophas by name, asked him, "Are you the only resident of Jerusalem who does not know the things that went on there these past few days?" He said to them, "What things?" They said: "All those that had to do with Jesus of Nazareth, a prophet powerful in word and deed in the eyes of God and all the people, how our chief priests and leaders delivered Him up to be condemned to death, and crucified him. We were hoping that He was the one who would set Israel free. Besides all this, today, the third day since these things happened, some women of our group have just brought us some astonishing news. They were at the tomb before dawn and failed to find his body, but returned with the tale that they had a vision of angels who declared he was alive. Some of our number went to the tomb and found it to be just as the women said, but him they did not see." Then he said to them," What little sense you have! How slow you are to believe all that the prophets have announced! Did not the Messiah have to undergo all this so as to enter into his Glory?" Beginning then with Moses and all the prophets, He interpreted for them every passage of Scripture, which referred to him. By now they were near the village to which they were going, and he acted as if he were going farther. But they pressed him: "Stay with us. It

The two disciples speak with Jesus on the road to Emmaus without knowing Him.

is nearly evening - the day is practically over." So he went in to stay with them. When he had seated himself with them to eat, he took bread, pronounced the blessing, then broke the bread and began to distribute it to them. With that their eyes were opened and they recognized Him; whereupon he vanished from their sight. They said to one another, "Were not our hearts burning inside us as he talked to us on the road and explained the Scriptures to us?" They got up immediately and retuned to Jerusalem, where they found the Eleven and the rest of the company assembled. They were greeted with, "The Lord has been raised! It is true! He has appeared to Simon." Then they recounted what had happened on the road and how they had come to know Him in the Breaking of the Bread.

Reflection

Emmaus is located west of Jerusalem and the two men where walking into the sunset which suggests the reason for not recognizing Jesus. However, that may be true, but the man of faith is one who walks not towards the sunset but toward the sunrise. Our faith goes onward, not to a night which falls, but to a dawn which breaks and that is what, in their sorrow and their disappointment, the two men on the Emmaus road had not realized.

This reading tells us of the ability of Jesus to make sense of things, which we don't understand. The whole situation seemed to these two men to have no explanation. Their hopes and dreams were shattered, like many times ours are. We were hoping that he was the one who was going to rescue Israel, they said. Yes, they were the words of these men whose hopes were dead and buried. Then Jesus came and talked with them, and the meaning of life became clear and the darkness became light to them. It is only in Jesus that, even in the bewildering times, we learn what life means.

Emmaus – About seven miles from Jerusalem is El-Qubeibe the old Roman Road to Emmaus, where the traditional site for the house of Cleopas is located.

We also see the courtesy of Jesus in this reading. He gave the impression as if he would have gone on. He would not force himself upon them; he waited their invitation to come in. God gave to us the greatest and the most precious gift in the world, the gift of free-will; we can use it to invite Christ to enter our own lives or to allow him to pass on. The choice is ours.

Prayer

Lord Jesus, walk with us on our way. Let your words burn within us so that our hearts may never grow cold. Awaken us to the reality of your presence in your life-giving Word, and in the breaking of the bread.

Inspirational thoughts

If God brings you to it, He will bring you through it.

We must make our homes centers of compassion and forgive endlessly.

Do not allow yourself to be disheartened by any failures as long as you have done your best.

Feed your faith and your doubts will starve to death.

To forgive is to set the prisoner free, and then discover the prisoner was you.

The shortest distance between a problem and a solution is the distance between your knees and the floor. The one who kneels to the Lord can stand up to anything.

God wants spiritual fruit, not religious nuts!!

Fate is what we are compelled to do; destiny is what we are meant to do.

It's not the problems in life that matter, but how we react to them.

It's not the money we have, but how we spend it.

It's not about the time we have, but how we spend that time.

It's not the size of your plate, but what's on your plate that really matters.

God will use you to touch other people if you only let Him.

The light you are may be the only light some people ever see.

In a little while it will be eternity!

God can use you while you're still changing.

They say it takes a minute to find a special person, an hour to appreciate them, a day to love them, but an entire lifetime to forget them.

God is more interested in changing you than your circumstances.

Adversity does not build character....it reveals it!

Sometimes in the waves of change we find our true direction!

God won't ask the square footage of your house, but He'll ask how many people you welcomed into your home.

God won't ask how many material possessions you received, but He'll ask if they dictated your life.

God won't ask how many friedns you had, but He'll ask how many people to whom you were a friend.

PUSH= Pray Until Something Happens.

ASAP= Always Say A Prayer.

You may be only one person in the world, but you may also be the world to one person.

Don't cry because it's over; smile because it happened.

The will of God never takes you where the grace of God will not protect you.

It's not <u>what</u> you have in your life, but <u>whom</u> your have in your life that matters.

CHAPTER 7
JERICHO AREA
(Jericho, Samaria, Jordan River)

Jericho- Zacchaeus
Luke 19: 1-10

Blind Man at Jericho
Luke 18: 35-43

Good Samaritan
Luke 10: 25-38

Moses View of the Promised Land
Deuteronomy 34

Jesus has no place to lay his head
Luke 9: 57-62

Fig Tree
Luke 13: 6-9

Baptism of Jesus
Matthew 3: 13-17

St. John The Baptist Death
Mark 6: 14-29

The Cracked Water Pot Story

Samaria

Jacob's Well
John 4: 4-26

Cure of the Lepers
Luke 17: 11-19

Sycamore Tree in Jericho.

JERICHO- AN OASIS

Jericho was a very wealthy and important town. It lay in the Jordan valley and commanded both the approach to Jerusalem and crossings of the river, which gave access to the lands east of the Jordan. Josephus called it " a divine region," the fattest in Palestine." It had a great palm forest and world famous balsam groves. Jericho is the oldest city on earth and also the lowest point on earth. The numerous vendors that sells freshly squeezed orange and lemon juices add to the heighten impression of an oasis.

Luke 19: 1-10 Jesus entered Jericho and was passing through it. There was a man called Zacchaeus by name, and he was commissioner of taxes, and a wealthy man. He was seeking to see who Jesus was, and he could not for the crowd, because he was short in stature. So he ran on ahead and climbed up into a Sycamore tree, for He was to pass that way. When Jesus came to the place he looked up and said to him, "Zacchaeus! Hurry and come down! For this very day I must stay at your house." So he hurried and came down, and welcomed Him gladly; and when they saw it they all murmured, " He was gone in to be the guest of a man who is a sinner." Zacchaeus stood and said to the Lord, "Behold, half of my possessions, Lord, I shall give to the poor, "Lord, If I have taken anything from any man by fraud I give it back to him four times over." Jesus said to him, "Today salvation has come to this house, because he also is a son of Abraham; for the Son of Man came to seek and to save that which was lost."

REFLECTION

Interesting enough Zacchaeus was a wealthy man but yet was not happy. We see Zacchaeus reaching after and finding the love of God. He was determined to see Jesus and would let nothing stop him. He also showed the community that he was a changed man and went beyond the necessary restitution to prove this. By his deeds he showed everyone that he was truly a changed man. You see it is not a mere change of words, which Jesus Christ demands, but a change of life. This story ends with the greatest of words, "The Son of Man came to seek and to save that which was lost". A man

Jericho and Mt of Temptation – And Jesus full of the Holy Spirit,
returned from the Jordan, and was led by the spirit for forty
days in the wilderness, tempted by the devil. Luke 4: 1-2.

is only lost when he has wandered away from God, and he is found when once again he takes his rightful place as an obedient child in the household and the family of God. Can we ask ourselves do we have the courage of Zacchaeus in our own lives?

Luke 18:35-43 When Jesus was approaching Jericho, a blind man was sitting by the wayside begging. When he heard the crowd passing through he asked what it meant? They told him, "Jesus of Nazareth is passing by." He shouted, "Jesus, Son of David, have pity on me!" Those who were going on in front rebuked him and

Qumran & Dead Sea Scrolls These are the cave in which the Dead Sea Scrolls where found by two Bedouin shepherds.

The Samaritan dresses the wounds of the injured man.

told him to be quiet, but he cried all the more, "Son of David, have pity on me." Jesus stood, and ordered him to be brought to him. When he had come near he asked him, " What do you want me to do for you?" He said, " Lord, that I may receive my sight." Jesus said to him, "Receive your sight; your faith has made you well." And immediately he received his sight and followed Him glorifying God, and, when the people saw it, they all gave praise to God.

REFLECTION

It was a common practice for a Rabbi to teach along the way and this is exactly what Jesus was doing at the time, when He met the blind man. Jesus shows us that it is always more important to act than to talk and words take second place to good deeds. Here was a human soul in need of help and Jesus reached out to him. How often have we seen someone who can't put two sentences together, but yet people love him because he is so kind. We may respect a great speaker, but we really love a person with helping hands. We may admire a person with a great mind, but we always love someone who has a big heart. Let us pray that Jesus will give us the spiritual sight and sound to see and hear him in the poor and suffering.

GOOD SAMARITAN

Luke 10: 25-38 On one occasion a lawyer stood up to pose him this problem: "Teacher, what must I do to inherit everlasting life?" Jesus answered him: "What is written in the law? How do you read it?" He replied: "You shall love the Lord your God with all your heart, with all your soul, with all your strength, and with all your mind; and your neighbor as yourself." Jesus said, "You have answered correctly. Do this and you shall live." But because he wished to justify himself he said to Jesus, " And who is my neighbor?" Jesus replied: A man fell victim to robbers as he went down from Jerusalem to Jericho. They stripped and beat him and went off leaving him half dead. A priest happened to be going down that road, but when he saw him, he passed by on the opposite side. Likewise a Levite came to the place, and when he saw him, he passed by on the opposite side. But a Samaritan traveler who came upon him was moved with compassion at the sight. He approached the victim, poured oil and wine over his wounds and bandaged them. Then he lifted him up on his own animal, took him to an inn and cared for him. The next day he took out two silver coins and gave them to the innkeeper with the instructions, "Take care of him. If you spend more than what I have given you, I shall repay you on my way back." Which of these three, in your opinion, was neighbor to the robbers victim?" He answered, " The one who treated him with mercy." Jesus said to him, "Go and do likewise".

REFLECTION

When Jesus told this story, he was telling about the kind of thing that was constantly happening on the Jerusalem to Jericho Road. There was the priest who no doubt was remembering that he who touched a dead man was unclean for seven days. There was the Levite who seemed to have gone nearer to the man before he too, passed by. Then there was a Samaritan, a name used to describe a man who was a heretic, and breaker of the ceremonial law. A heretic he may have been, but the love of God was in his heart. It is no new experience to find the orthodox more interested in dogmas than in help, and to find the man the orthodox despise to be the one who loves his fellow man. In the end, we will be judged not by the creed

Jericho.

we hold, but by the life we live. No doubt the priest and the Levite felt pity for the wounded man, but they did nothing. Compassion, to be real must result in some type of kind act. What Jesus said to the scribe, he says to each of us: "Go you and do the same".

VIEW OF JERICHO BY MOSES

Deuteronomy 34 "Then Moses went up from the plains of Moab to Mt. Nebo, which faces Jericho, and the Lord showed him all the land. The Lord then said to him, "This is the land, which I swore to Abraham, Isaac and Jacob, that I would give to their descendents. I have let you feast your eyes on it, but you shall not cross over." So there Moses died. Since then, no prophet has arisen in Israel like Moses, whom the Lord knew face to face."

You shall have no gods except me.

You shall not utter the name of
Yahweh your God to misuse it.

Remember the sabbath day and keep
it holy.

Honour your father and your mother.

You shall not kill.

You shall not commit adultery.

You shall not steal.

You shall not bear false witness against
your neighbour.

You shall not covet your neighbour's
house.

You shall not covet your neighbour's
wife, or anything that is his.

REFLECTION

There are three things we can learn from this reading and Moses. 1.) Moses learned early that violence was not the way to solve problems. 2.) In order for Moses to find God in his life he had to go by himself into the desert. How true this is of our own spiritual lives. 3.) He also learned that he could lead people only so far spiritually, and then God will take over. We can lead you only so far on this trip and then the rest will be up to you and how you react to God's grace.

Luke 9: 57-62 As they were journeying along the road, a man said to Jesus, "I will follow you wherever you go." Jesus said to him, "the foxes have dens; the birds of the air have places to roost; but the Son of Man has nowhere to lay his head." He said to another man, "Follow Me!" "Lord", he said, "let me go first and bury my father." He said to him, "Let the dead bury their dead; but do you go and tell abroad the news of the kingdom of God." Another man said to him, "Lord, I will follow you, but let me first say good-bye to the folks at home." Jesus said to him, "No man who puts his hand to the plough and looks back is the right kind of man for the kingdom of God.

REFLECTION

Jesus was making the point that there is a crucial moment in everyone's life, and if we miss this movement most likely that moment will be lost forever. The man in the story has stirrings in his heart to get out of his spiritually dead surroundings, and if he missed that moment he would never get out. Our Christian belief marches on, not to the sunset, but to the dawn. I also wonder if when St. Peter was being crucified upside down in Rome that he ever thought that had he kept his mouth closed he could have died as a simple fisherman on the beautiful Sea of Galilee. We know the history of Peter's life,

Judean Desert.

and his decision to follow Jesus. It's so true of our lives: if we make a commitment to follow Jesus we cannot look backward just forward.

Luke 13: 6-9 Jesus spoke this parable, " A man had a fig-tree planted in his vineyard. He came looking for fruit on it and did not find it. He said to the keeper of the vineyard, "Look you-for the last three years I have been coming and looking for fruit on this

Fig Tree – located near Jericho.

fig-tree, and I still am not finding any. Cut it down! Why should it use up the ground? "Lord, he answered him, Let it be this year too, until I dig round about it and manure it, and if it bears fruit in the coming year, well and good; if not, you will cut it down."

REFLECTION

The parable teaches that nothing, which only takes out, can survive. The fig tree was drawing nutrition, fertilizer, and water out of the soil; in return was producing nothing. That is exactly like its sin. Remember that life is a measure to be filled, not a cup to be drained.

I guess we can say there are two kinds of people in this world- those who take out more than they put in, and those who put in more than they take out. Which are we?

RENEWAL OF BAPTISMAL PROMISES

Do you reject sin so as to live in the freedom of God's children?

I do.

Do you reject the glamor of evil, and refuse to be mastered by sin?

I do.

Do you reject Satan, father of sin and prince of darkness?

I do.

Do you reject Satan?

I do.

And all his works?

I do.

And all his empty promises?

I do.

Do you believe in God, the Father almighty, creator of heaven and earth?

I do.

Do you believe in Jesus Christ, his only Son, our Lord, who was born of the Virgin Mary, was crucified, died, and was buried, rose from the dead, and is seated at the right hand of the Father?

I do.

Do you believe in the Hoy Spirit, the holy catholic Church, the communion of saints, the forgiveness of sins, the resurrection of the body, and life everlasting?

I do.

(Sprinkle each other with some of the water from the Jordan
    River)

BAPTISM OF JESUS IN THE JORDAN RIVER

**Matthew 3:13-17 Then Jesus came from Galilee to John at the
Jordan to be baptized by him. John tried to prevent him, saying,
"I need to be baptized by You, and yet You are coming to me?"
Jesus said to him in reply, "Allow it now, for thus it is fitting for
us to fulfill all righteousness." Then he allowed Him. After Jesus
was baptized, He came up from the water and behold, the heavens
were opened and He saw the Spirit of God descending like a dove
coming upon Him. And a voice came from the heavens, saying,
"This is my beloved Son, with whom I am well pleased."**

REFLECTION

When Jesus came to John to be baptized, John was startled and
unwilling to baptize Him. It was John's conviction that it was he
who needed what Jesus could give, not Jesus who needed what he
could give. From the earliest times scholars were puzzled by the
fact that Jesus submitted to be baptized. But there were reasons,
and good reasons, why he did. For thirty years Jesus had waited in
Nazareth, faithfully performing the simple duties of a carpenter. All
the time He knew that a world was waiting for him. All the time He
grew increasingly conscious of His waiting task. The success of any
undertaking is determined by the wisdom with which the moment
to embark upon it is chosen. Jesus must have waited for the hour to
strike, for the moment to come, and when John emerged, then Jesus
knew that the time had arrived.

Why should that be so? There was one very simple and very

vital reason. It is the fact that never in all history before this had any Jew submitted to being baptized. The Jews knew and used baptism, but only for converts who came into Judaism from some other faith. It was natural that the sin stained, polluted convert should be baptized, but no Jew had ever conceived that he, as a member of the chosen people, a son of Abraham, assured of God's salvation, could ever need baptism.

So in this baptism there came to Jesus two certainties – the certainty that He was indeed the chosen One of God, and the certainty that the way in front of Him was the way of the Cross. In that moment He knew that He was chosen to be King, but He also knew that His throne must be a Cross. In that moment He knew that He was destined to be a conqueror, but that His conquest must have as its only weapon the power of suffering love. In that moment there was set before Jesus both his task and the only way to fulfill it.

We do not know the certainty of our own lives. We all have traveled here in faith and still have questions about our own future. Be certain in the fact that in order to see the tomb and the resurrection we first need to pass by Calvary. Take time and enjoy the Jordan River.

ST. JOHN THE BAPTIST DEATH

Mark 6: 14-29 King Herod came to hear of Jesus whose reputation had become widespread and people were saying, John the Baptizer has been raised from the dead; that is why such miraculous powers are at work in him." Others were saying, "He is Elijah"; still others, "He is a prophet equal to any of the prophets." On hearing of Jesus, Herod exclaimed, "John, whose head I had cut off, has been raised up!" Herod was the one who had ordered John arrested, chained,

*Jordan River – The river begins some 950 feet above sea level, descends to
the Sea of Galilee, which is 680 feet below sea level, and continues to
descent toward the Dead Sea whose surface is 1340 feet below sea level.
The Baptism of Jesus by John took place here in the Jordan River.*

and imprisoned on account of Herodias, the wife of his brother
Philip, whom he had married. That was because John had told
Herod, "It is not right for you to live with your brother's wife."
Herodias harbored a grudge against him for this and wanted to kill
him but was unable to do so. Herod feared John, knowing him to be
an upright and holy man, and kept him in custody. When he heard
him speak he was very much disturbed; yet he felt the attraction
of his words. Herodias has her chance one day when Herod held a
birthday dinner for his court circle, military officers, and the leading
men of Galilee. Herodias' own daughter came in at one point and

performed a dance, which delighted Herod and his guests. The king told the girl, "Ask for anything you want and I will grant you whatever you ask, even to half my kingdom!" She went out and said to her mother, "What shall I ask for?" The mother answered, "The head of John the Baptizer." At that the girl hurried back to the king's presence and made her request: "I want you to give me, at once, the head of John the Baptzer on a platter." The king bitterly regretted the request; yet because of his oath and the presence of the guests, he did not want to refuse her. He promptly dispatched an executioner, ordering him to bring back the Baptizer's head. The man went and beheaded John in the prison. He brought in the head on a platter and gave it to the girl, and the girl gave it to her mother. Later, when his disciples heard about this, they came and carried his body away and laid it in a tomb.

REFLECTION

Machaerus stood on a lonely ridge, surrounded by steep ravines, overlooking the east side of the Dead Sea. It was one of the loneliest and grimmest and most unassailable fortresses in the world. To this day the dungeons are there and you can see the staples and the iron hooks in the wall to which John must have been bound. It was at this desolate place that John met his death. In spite of John's rebuke Herod still feared and respected him, for John was so obviously a man of sincerity and of goodness, but with Herodias (his so called wife) it was different. She was determined to eliminate him. Herod was a man who acted on impulse. It may be that he had too much to drink and was more than a little drunk. Let every person think before he speaks. Let us never by self –indulgence get into a state when we lose our powers of judgment, and are liable to do things for which afterwards we will be very sorry. They say that a good woman

The head of John the Baptist is brought to the daughter of Herodias.

might marry a bad man, for by so doing she would end by making him as good as herself. But they also say that a good man might never marry a bad woman, for she would inevitable drag him down to her own level. The trouble with Herodias was that she wished to eliminate the one man who had the courage to confront her with her sin. She wished to do as she like with no regard to her moral life. She murdered John so that she might sin in peace. She forgot that while she longer will meet John, she still had to meet God. St. John the Baptist preferred death to falsehood. . He lived for the truth and he died for it. Let us all pray that we too have the courage and the strength of St. John the Baptist in our struggle with truth.

CRACKED WATER POT STORY

The story was about a man who was water carrier in Biblical times near Jericho. In Vietnam I used to see the men carry water in clay pots hung on each end of a pole carried across their necks and shoulders. During one of my visits to Israel I recalled a story that brought this image to life. Each day the water bearer would go down to the local watering hole to gather water for his master's house. One of the pots had a crack in it, and while the other pot was perfect and always delivered a full portion of water at the end of the long walk from the stream to the master's house. The cracked pot arrived only half full. The story goes that this went on daily for nearly two years, whereby the water carrier would deliver only one and one half pots of water each day to the master's house. Of course, the perfect pot was proud of its accomplishments, perfect to the end for which it was made. But the poor cracked pot was ashamed of its own imperfection, and miserable that it was able to accomplish only half of what it had been made to do. After two years of what it perceived to be a bitter failure, it spoke to the water bearer one day by the stream. "I am ashamed of myself, and I want to apologize to you." "Why?" asked the water bearer. "What are you ashamed of"? "I have been able, for these two years, to deliver only half my water because this crack in my side causes water to leak out all the way back to your master's house. Because of my flaws, you have to do all of this work, and you don't get full value from your efforts," the pot said. The water bearer felt sorry for the old cracked pot, and in his compassion he said, "As we return to the master's house, I want you to notice the beautiful flowers along the path". But at the end of the trail, the cracked pot still felt bad because it had leaked out half its load, and so again it apologized to the bearer for its failure. The bearer said to the pot, "Did you notice that there were flowers only on your side of your path, but not on the other pot's side? **That's because I have always known about your flaw, and I took advantage of it**. I planted flower seeds on your side of the path, and every day while we walk back from the stream, you've watered them. For two years I have been able to pick these beautiful flowers to decorate my master's table. **Without you being just the way you are**, my master would not have this beauty to grace his house.

Each of us has our own unique flaws. We're all cracked pots. In God's great beauty, nothing goes to waste. **Man is broken and the grace of God is the glue that holds it together.**

WHO WERE THE SAMARITANS?

Samaritans were a mixed group, believed to have been the descendants of intermarriages between Jews and local Gentiles, notably the Philistines, Edomites, Syrians, and Moabites. The Samaritans had a relatively simple faith, almost that of the Jews, but using only the Torah (five books of Moses), rejecting the "writings" (Psalms and other historic, poetic, and metaphorical works) and the "prophets" (Isaiah,

Jeremiah, and so forth to Malachi). Their worship focused towards a mountain in Samaria rather than the mountain in Jerusalem, and their version of the Torah differed from the Jewish Torah in naming this mountain as the center of their worship.

So what were Samaritans to Jews? They were considered better than Gentiles, but inferior to Jews. They were permitted to travel rather freely in the two parts of Israel because the Israelites themselves were often constrained to pass through Samaria on their way from one part to the other. However, Jews and Samaritans did not mix, socially. The Jews did not want to risk their social position by being associated with inferior persons, and the Samaritans wanted as little as possible to do with the snobbish Jews who thought themselves better than they.

JACOB'S WELL READING

John 4: 4-26 He had to pass through Samaria. So He came to a town of Samaria called Sychar, near the plot of land that Jacob had given to his son Joseph. Jacob's well was there. Jesus, tired from His journey, sat down there at the well. It was about noon. A woman of Samaria came to draw water. Jesus said to her, "Give me a drink." His disciples had gone into the town to buy food. The Samaritan woman said to Him, "How can you, a Jew, ask me, a Samaritan woman, for a drink?" (For Jews use nothing in common with Samaritans.) Jesus answered and said to her, "If you knew the gift of God and who is saying to you, "Give me a drink, you would have asked him and He would have given you living water." The woman said to Him, "Sir, You do not even have a bucket and the cistern is deep; where then can you get this living water? Are you greater than our father Jacob, who gave us this cistern and drank from it himself with his children and his flocks?" Jesus answered

Jacob's Well – A Greek Orthodox church was built here, with the well in the center of its crypt. It was at this well that Jesus met the Samaritan woman and asked her for water to drink. "Every one who drinks of this water will thirst again, but whoever drinks of the water that I shall give him will never thirst; John 4: 13-14.

and said to her, "Everyone who drinks this water will be thirsty again; but whoever drinks the water I shall give will never thirst; the water I shall give will become in him a spring of water welling up to eternal life. The woman said to Him, "Sir, give me this water, so that I may not be thirsty or have to keep coming here to draw water." Jesus said to her, "Go call your husband and come back." The woman answered and said to Him, "I do not have a husband." Jesus answered her, "You are right in saying, I do not have a husband. For you have had five husbands, and the one you have now is not your husband. What you have said is true. The woman said to Him, "Sir, I can see that you are a prophet. Our

Jesus tells the Samaritan woman about the living water that He will give to men.

ancestors worshiped on this mountain, but you people say that the place to worship is in Jerusalem." Jesus said to her, "Believe me, woman, the hour is coming when you will worship the Father neither on this mountain nor in Jerusalem. You people worship what you do not understand; we worship what we understand, because salvation is from the Jews. But the hour is coming, and is now here, when true worshipers will worship the Father in Spirit and truth; and indeed the Father seeks such people to worship Him. God is Spirit, and those who worship Him must worship in Spirit and truth." The woman said to him, "I know that the Messiah is coming, the one called the Anointed; when He comes, He will tell us everything. Jesus said to her, "I am He, the one who is speaking with you."

REFLECTION

The well itself was more than 100 feet deep and it is a well, in which the water percolates and gathers so you need a bucket with a long rope on it to draw up the water. I think that this Samaritan woman must have unburdened her soul to this stranger. It was probably one of the few times in her life that she found someone with kindness in His eyes and she opened her heart to Him. She had at last met someone who was not a critic but a friend, One who did not condemn but Who understood. Jesus is seen breaking down all the barriers. The quarrel between the Jews and the Samaritans was an old story, which lasted for more than 400 years. Jesus was talking to a woman. It was strictly forbidden by any Rabbi to greet a woman in public. Not only was she a woman; she was also a woman of notorious character. Here was the holiest of men, listening with understanding and compassion to a sad story; Jesus breaking through the barriers of nationally and orthodox Jewish custom. Here is God so loving the world, not in theory, but in action. There is a certain thirst we all have, but which only Jesus Christ can satisfy.

Luke 17: 11-19 When Jesus was on the way to Jerusalem, He was going along between Samaria and Galilee, and as He entered a village, ten lepers, who stood far off who met Him. They lifted up their voices and said, "Jesus, Master have pity upon us." When He saw them, He said, " Go and show yourself to the priests." And as they went they were cleansed. One of them when he saw that he was cured turned back, glorifying God with a great voice. He fell on his face at Jesus' feet and kept on thanking Him, and he was a Samaritan. Jesus said," were the ten not cleansed? The nine where are they? Were none found to turn back and give glory to God except this foreigner?" And He said to him, "rise and go! Your faith has made you well."

REFLECTION

Here is an example of a great law of life. If only we could remember it in our own life. In the common tragedy of their leprosy they had forgotten they were Jews and Samaritans and remembered only they were men in need. One of the biggest things, which should draw all men together, is their common need of God. So often in life, once a man has gotten what he wants, he never comes back. Often we are ungrateful to our parents and still worse we are often ungrateful to God. We sometimes get leprosy of the heart and forget to thank God for all the good things that come to us daily, which we fail to recognize. Let us pray that we never forget the source of all love, which is God.

There were ten lepers who were cured, but only one leper returns and thanks Jesus for making him well.

*Samarian Farmer –
Samaria is a mountainous
region located between
Judea and Galilee between
the coastal plain in the
west and the Jordan
Valley in the east.*

MOUNT OF TEMPTATION
JERICHO

Matthew 4:1-4 and 8-11 Then Jesus was led into the desert by the Spirit to be tempted by the devil. He fasted forty days and forty nights, and afterward was hungry. The tempter approached and said to him, "If you are the Son of God, command these stones to turn into bread." Jesus replied, "Scripture has it: Not on bread alone is man to live, but on every utterance that comes from the mouth of God."

The devil then took him up a very high mountain and displayed before him all the kingdoms of the world in their magnificence, promising, "All these will I bestow on you if you prostrate yourself in homage before me." At this Jesus said to him, "Away with you, Satan! Scripture has it: You shall do homage to the Lord your God; him alone shall you adore." At that the devil left him, and angels came and waited on him.

REFLECTION

Just as metal has to be tested far beyond any stress and strain that it will ever be called upon to bear, before it can be put to any useful purpose, so we too have to be tested before God can use us for His purpose". These tests are not meant to make us bad, they are meant to make us good. They are not meant to weaken us, they are meant to make us emerge stronger and finer and purer from any ordeal. Temptations are not the penalty of being a man or woman, but temptations are the glory of being a human being. It is the test which comes to each of us whom God wishes to use. So we shouldn't look at this whole incident as the tempting of Jesus, but the testing of Jesus. Sometimes people think that they reached a stage in their life which is beyond temptation, a stage at which the power of the devil is forever broken. Jesus never reached that stage in life and neither will we. Remember Jesus was tempted near the end of his life in the Garden of Gethsemane so as to deflect him from the Cross. We will all be faced with temptation even toward the end of our lives. The important thing is how we respond to it. We all should lead a life of prayer so that we can be victorious in our battle with temptation even to our dying breath. St. John Vianney once said, "that we should beware when we are not tempted because that means that the devil regards us as his own".

CHAPTER 8
NAZARETH

Annunciation
Luke 1: 26-38

The Angelus

St. Joseph Dream
Matthew 1: 18-24

Nazareth Synagogue
Mark 6: 1-6
Luke 4: 16-30

Cana- Wedding Feast
John 2: 1-11

Divorce
Mark 10: 1-3

Mt. Tabor – Transfiguration
Matthew 17: 1-9
Mark 9: 14-29 (Coming Down Mt. Tabor)

Naim-boy brought back to life
Luke 7: 11-17

Church of the Annunciation – This is the present Basilica of the Annunciation, which was dedicated on March 25, 1969. The Basilica was visited by Pope Paul VI during his visit to the Holy Land in 1964. The top of the Basilica represents an inverted lily symbolic of the graces coming from God down upon Our Lady.

Luke 1: 26-38 In the sixth month, the angel Gabriel was sent from God to a town of Galilee named Nazareth, to a virgin betrothed to a man named Joseph, of the house of David. The virgin's name was Mary. Upon arriving the angel said to her: "Rejoice, O highly favored daughter! The Lord is with you. Blessed are you among women." She was deeply troubled by his words, and wondered what his greeting meant. The angel went on to say to her:" Do not fear, Mary. You have found favor with God. You shall conceive and bear a Son and give Him the name Jesus. Great will be His dignity and He will be called Son of the Most High. The Lord

The Angel Gabriel says to Mary, "Hail, full of grace! The Lord is with you."

God will give Him the throne of David His father. He will rule over the house of Jacob forever and His reign will be without end." Mary said to the angel, "How can this be since I do not know man?" The angel answered her: "The Holy Spirit will overshadow you; hence, the Holy Offspring to be born will be called Son of God. Know that Elizabeth your kinswoman has conceived a son in her old age; she who was thought to be sterile is now in her sixth month, for nothing is impossible with God." Mary said: " I am the servant of the Lord. Let it be done to me as you say." With that the angel left her.

REFLECTION

Mary's submission is a very lovely thing to hear. Mary has learned to pray the world's greatest prayer which is " Thy will be done." It is here that God chose the loveliest creature of them all, a young girl name Mary. God poured into the child of her womb His divinity. This was incredible and hard to understand mystery. It is a great gift and a mystery of the highest caliber. The greatest thing that ever happened in the history of the world happened in the womb of Mary. God became Man. Actually this is the spot where we actually received the Our Father prayer, because it was here that the Word was made flesh. It was at this point in history, where God the Father truly became Our Father. In the light of Divine Providence, if we observe carefully, we will see that "God writes straight with crooked lines." We may not know what He is up to, but He does.

THE ANGELUS

The Angel of the Lord declared unto Mary
Response: And she conceived of the Holy Spirit.
(Hail Mary full of grace…)

Behold the handmaid of the Lord
Response: Be it done unto me according to thy word.
(Hail Mary full of grace….)

And the word was made flesh,
Response: And dwelt among us.
(Hail Mary full of grace….)

Pray for us, O Holy Mother of God,
Response: That we may be made worthy of the promises of Christ.

Grotto of the Annunciation – The grotto, the holiest spot in the church edifice, which is lighted by a copper canopy above it. The nearby remains of previous churches demonstrate the antiquity of the tradition that the Annunciation of Mary took place here.

Let us pray: *Pour forth, we beseech You, O Lord, Thy grace into our hearts, that we to whom the Incarnation of Christ, Thy Son, was made known by the message of an angel, may His passion and cross be brought to the glory of His Resurrection, through the same Christ Our Lord. Amen*

Read at the Church of the Annunciation
MEDITATION

When the darkness of sin covered mankind, your love and humility, kind Mother, turned the face of the Father toward His erring children. Though the message of the Angel was difficult for you to understand, you accepted the Will of God with trust and love. You questioned neither His Power nor His Wisdom, but asked only how this great Mystery was to be accomplished. We live in a world that does not trust in His Providence, does not believe in His Power.

Your trust in the Father's Will made the miraculous simple. Why can't we trust His plan in our lives as you trusted Him in yours? Even though the child born to be the Savior would suffer untold agonies, you never for a moment hesitated in your Fiat. The women of our day fear the future of their unborn children. In an act of misguided zeal they sometimes deprive the Father of the opportunity to manifest His Power, bestow upon us His Goodness and populate the Kingdom with children of light.

Give us a share of your Faith and Hope that we may bow before the Infinite Wisdom of God and accept the treasures He deigns to bestow upon us. Let us leave creation to His Omnipotence, the future to His Providence and mankind to His Wisdom.

SONG: ON THIS DAY

Refrain:
On this day, O beautiful Mother,
On this day, we give thee our love
Near thee, Madonna, fondly we hover,
Trusting thy gentle care to prove.
On this day we ask to share
Dearest Mother, thy sweet care
Aid us ere our feet astray
Wander from thy guiding way.
Refrain:
Queen of angels, deign to hear
Lisping children's humble prayers
Young hearts gain, O Virgin pure
Sweetly to thyself allure.
Refrain:

Matthew 1: 18-24 This is how the birth of Jesus Christ came about. When his mother Mary was betrothed to Joseph, but before they lived together, she was found with child through the Holy Spirit. Joseph her husband, since he was a righteous man, yet unwilling to expose her to shame, decided to divorce her quietly. Such was his intention when, behold, the angel of the Lord appeared to him in a dream and said, "Joseph, son of David, do not be afraid to take Mary your wife into your home. For it is through the Holy Spirit that this Child has been conceived in her. She will bear a son and you are to name him Jesus, because He will save His people from their sins". All this took place to fulfill what the Lord had said through the prophet: "Behold, the virgin shall conceive and bear a son, and they shall name him Emmanuel," which means "God is with us". When Joseph awoke, he did as the angel of the Lord had commanded him, and took his wife into his home.

REFLECTION

Joseph was pious and just in the eyes of God, and realized that Mary was special and destined to do great things. Joseph did not want to interfere with God's plans, and planned to quietly divorce Mary. It wasn't until the angel appeared to him in a dream, that he realized that he too was also part of God's plan. How true it is of our own lives, that God is calling each and every one of us and we are also part of his plan. God will use you to touch other people if you just let him.

PRAYER

Remember, O most pure spouse of Mary, and my dearly beloved guardian, St. Joseph, that never was it known, that anyone who invoked your care and requested your help was left without consolation. Inspired

with this confidence, I come to you, and with all the ardor of my spirit I commend myself to you. Do not reject my prayer, Foster Father of the savior, but graciously receive and answer it. Amen
(St. Faustina wrote in her diary, "St. Joseph urged me to have a constant devotion to him. He himself told me to recite every day the "Remember" prayer. He has promised me his special help and protection.)

Matthew 11: 28-30 "Come to me, all you who are exhausted and weighted down beneath your burdens, and I will give you rest. Take my yoke upon you, and learn of me, for I am gentle and lowly in heart, and you will find rest for your souls; for my yoke is easy and my burden is light."

Church of St. Joseph in Nazareth. The stained glass window shows St. Joseph & the Blessed Mother joining hands in marriage by a Rabbi

REFLECTION

Jesus was speaking to men who were desperately trying to find God and desperately trying to be good very much like you guys are doing, but yet finding it difficult to do. Here Jesus invites us to take his yoke upon our shoulders. The Jews used this phase "the yoke" for entering into submission. They spoke of the yoke of the Law, or the yoke of God. Jesus says, "My yoke is easy." During the time of Christ the ox-yoke were made of wood and the ox was brought to a carpenter and measurements were taken. The yoke was then roughed out, and the ox was brought back to have the yoke fitted. The yoke was carefully adjusted, so that it would fit well, and not dig at the neck of the ox. The yoke was tailor-made to fit the ox. There is a legend that Jesus made the best ox yokes in all Galilee, and that from all over the country men came to him to buy the best yokes that money could buy. In those days as now the shop had their signs above the door; and it has been suggested that the sign above the door of the carpenter's shop in Nazareth may well have been : "**My yoke fits well**.". Can I ask you this question – Does your yoke that you have now need adjustment or does it fit well? Jesus say, "My yoke fits all, which means the life I give you is not a burden to injure you, but the task is made to measure to fit you. It is not that the burden is easy to carry, but it is laid on us in love and is meant to be carried in love, and love makes even the heaviest burden light.

There is a story which tells how a man came upon a little boy carrying a still smaller boy, on his back because he was lame. "That's a heavy burden for you to carry," said the man. "That's no burden" came the answer. "That's my little brother." The burden which is given in love and carried in love is always light.

WITHOUT HONOR IN HIS HOME TOWN IN THE SYNAGOGUE

Luke 4: 16-30 He came to Nazareth where he has been reared, and entering the synagogue on the Sabbath he was as he was in the habit of doing, he stood up to do the reading. When the book of the prophet Isaiah was handed Him, He unrolled the scroll and found the passage where it was written: "The spirit of the Lord is upon me; therefore He has anointed me. He has sent me to bring glad tidings to the poor, to proclaim liberty to captives, recovery of sight to the blind and release to prisoners, and to announce a year of favor from the Lord." Rolling up the scroll He gave it back to the assistant and sat down. All in the synagogue had their eyes fixed on him. Then He began by saying to them, "Today this scripture passage is fulfilled in your hearing." All who were present spoke favorably of Him; they marveled at the appealing discourse, which came from Mis lips. They also asked, "Is not this Joseph son?" He

The author in the Synagogue in Nazareth- This very old structure is the synagogue where Jesus first preached.

said to them, "You will doubtless quote Me the proverb, "Physician, heal yourself, " and say, "Do here in your own country the things we have heard you have done in Capernaum. But in fact," He went on, "no prophet gains acceptance in His native place. Indeed, let me remind you, there were many widows in Israel in the day of Elijah when the heavens remained closed for three and a half years and a great famine spread over the land. It was to none of these that Elijah was sent, but to a widow of Zarephath near Sidon. Recall, too, the many lepers in Israel in the time of Elisha the prophet; yet not one was cured except Naaman the Syrian." At these words the whole audience in the synagogue was filled with indignation. They rose up and expelled Him from the town, leading Him to the brow of the hill on which it was built and intending to hurl Him over the edge. But He went straight through there midst and walked away.

REFLECTION

One of Jesus' very early visits was to Nazareth his hometown. If you could climb to the hilltop above the town you can see an amazing panorama for miles around. Nazareth stood in a little hollow in the hills on the lower slopes of Galilee near the Plain of Jezreel. What angered the people the most was the apparent compliment that Jesus paid to the Gentiles. The Jews at this time were so sure that they were God's chosen people that they utterly despised all others. It was Jesus' habit to go to the synagogue on the Sabbath. There must have been many things with which He radically disagreed and which irritated him, but yet he went on. The worship in the synagogue might be far from perfect, but yet Jesus never omitted to join himself to God's worshipping people on God's day. It was the good news that Jesus wanted to bring them. He knew the wrath of God, but he wanted to show them the wrath of love.

LACK OF FAITH (NAZARETH SYNAGOGUE)

Mark 6: 1-6 Jesus went to His own part of the country followed by His disciples. When the Sabbath came He began to teach in the synagogue in a way that kept his large audience amazed. They said: "Where did He get all this? What kind of wisdom is He endowed with? How is it such miraculous deeds are accomplished by His hands? Isn't this the carpenter, the son of Mary, a brother of James, Judas and Simon? Aren't His sisters our neighbors here?" They found Him too much for them. Jesus response to all this was: "no prophet is without honor except in His native place, among His own kindred, and in His own house." He could work no miracle there, apart from curing a few who were sick by laying hands on them, so much did their lack of faith distress Him. He made the rounds of the neighboring villages instead, and spent His time teaching.

REFLECTION

The fact that they called Jesus Mary's son tells us that Joseph must have been dead. Jesus was only thirty-three when He died, and yet He did not leave Nazareth until He was thirty. Why this lingering in Nazareth while a world waited to be saved? The reason was that Joseph died young and Jesus took upon Himself to support His mother. The people of Nazareth for some reason despised Him because they knew His family. Sometimes we are too near people to see their greatness. The result of all this was that Jesus could do no mighty works in Nazareth. The atmosphere was wrong and there are some things that cannot be done unless the atmosphere is right. It is true in our everyday life, for example no person can be healed if he refuses to be healed. There never can be peace making in the wrong atmosphere, and if men have come together to hate, they will hate. If men have come together to refuse to understand they will misunderstand. If men have come together to see no other point of view but their own, they will see no other. There is a tremendous responsibility on us all that we can either help or hinder the work of Jesus of Nazareth. We can open the door wide to Him or we can slam it in his face. The choice is ours.

CANA
(Wedding Feast)

John 2: 1-11 On the third day there was a wedding at Cana in Galilee, and the mother of Jesus was there. Jesus and His disciples had likewise been invited to the celebration. At a certain point the wine ran out, and Jesus' mother told Him, " They have no more wine," Jesus replied, "Woman, how does this concern of yours involve Me? My hour has not yet come." His mother instructed those waiting on table, " Do whatever He tells you." As prescribed for Jewish ceremonial washings, there were at hand six stone water jars, each one holding fifteen to twenty-five gallons. "Fill those jars with water," Jesus ordered at which they filled them to the brim. "Now, he said, "draw some out and take it to the waiter in charge." They did as He instructed them. The waiter in charge tasted the water made wine, without knowing where it had come from; only the waiters knew since they had drawn the water. Then the waiter in charge called the groom over and remarked to him: "People usually serve the choice wine first; then when the guests have been drinking a while, a lesser vintage. What you have done is keep the choice wine until now." Jesus performed this first of His signs at Cana in Galilee. Thus did he reveal His glory, and his disciples believed in Him.

*Church at Cana – Red roof church symbolic of the miracle which took place in side.
Jesus' first miracle at the wedding feast of Cana, where he change water into wine.*

No one falls in love by choice — it is by CHANCE.
No one stays in love by chance — it is by WORK.
No one falls out of love by chance — it is by CHOICE.

Reflection

In any marriage I think that the love for each other may go dry over
time. In order to find this love again you have to go back to the
source of love and that is God.

Mary had the faith, which could trust even when she did not
understand. She did not know what Jesus was going to do, but she
was quite sure that he would do the right thing. In every life comes

periods of darkness or dryness, when we do not see or feel His presence. In every life comes things which are such that we do not see why they came or any meaning in them. Happy is the person who in such a case still trusts even when we cannot understand. A successful marriage isn't finding the right person – it's being the right person.

Prayer

We praise You Lord, for Your gentle plan draws together Your children who are married and in love for one another. Strengthen their hearts, so that they will keep faith with each other, please You in all things, and so come to the happiness of celebrating the sacrament of their marriage. We ask this through Christ our Lord. Amen

This is an ideal spot for couples to renew their marriage vows.

The priest says: Father, we come before you with the love for each other that you, yourself have placed in our hearts. Here, your son changed water into wine. Continue to change our relationship, so that we may grow ever more deeply in love. Help us to love one another as Jesus has loved us.

The man says:
I, _____, renew my taking of you, _____ to be my wife, I renew my promise to be true to you in good times and in bad, in sickness and in health. I renew my love for you and I will honor you all the days of my life.

The woman says:
I, _____, renew my taking of you, _____ to be my husband. I renew my promise to be true to you in good times and

in bad, in sickness and in health. I renew my love for you and I will honor you all the days of my life.

The priest says: You have renewed your consent before God and his Church. May the Lord in his goodness strengthen your consent and fill you with his blessings, in the Name of the Father, and of the Son and of the Holy Spirit. I now pronounce you husband and wife. You may now kiss your spouse.

Private Meditation

Do not doubt Me, My friend. Do not be irritated at your pain, your losses, your sickness, your enemies. View them as the means by which I guide you to Myself. A wise parent does not forbid the child ever to run for fear it may fall or ever to leave the yard for fear it may be lost or get hurt. The parent acts thus in love, and I act in much more perfect love. If opposition and affliction were not the food of your spiritual growth, I would never allow them to approach you, much less touch you. I send you nothing that is too heavy for you to bear. Everything is fitted precisely to your strength. If you realized My love for you, you would surely have confidence in Me. Before the world was made, I loved you. When there was no earth, no sun, no angels, I knew you were to be , when you would appear, what place you would have in My plan, how long you would live, what thoughts you would think and what prayers you would pray and I loved you. Time never was when I did not love you. My making you was the expression of My Infinite, eternal love, as the kiss you bestow in the expression of your finite love….

Taken from the book <u>Message of Merciful Love To Little Souls,</u> where Jesus talks to His beloved children.

MARRIAGE AND DIVORCE

Mark 10: 1-13 He set out from there and went into the district of Judea. Again crowds gathered around Him, and as was His custom, He again taught them. The Pharisees approached and asked, "Is it lawful for a husband to divorce his wife?" They were testing him. He said to them in reply, "What did Moses command you?" They replied, "Moses permitted him to write a bill of divorce and dismiss her. But Jesus told them, "Because of the hardness of your hearts he wrote you this commandment. But from the beginning of creation, "God made them male and female for this reason: a man shall leave his father and mother and be joined to his wife, and the two shall become one flesh.

So they are no longer two but one flesh. Therefore what God has joined together, no human being must separate." In the house the disciples again questioned him about this. He said to them "Whoever divorces his wife and marries another commits adultery against her; and if she divorces her husband and marries another, she commits adultery."

REFLECTION

The Pharisees came with a question about divorce, by which they hoped to test Him or they wished for Jesus' opinion on the subject. It may be that these Pharisees had the hope that He might contradict himself and entangle Himself in His own words. One thing is certain the question they asked Jesus was no academic one of interest only to the rabbinic schools. It was a question, which dealt with all of humanity, and even affects each one of us today. In theory nothing could be higher than the Jewish ideal of marriage, and chastity was held to be the greatest of all the virtues. The woman at that time had no legal rights whatever, but was at the complete disposal of the male head of the family. The result was that a man could divorce his wife on almost any grounds, while there were very few grounds on which a woman could seek divorce. At best she could only ask her husband to divorce her. A woman may be divorced with or without her will, but a man only with his will. The only grounds on which a woman could claim a divorce were if her husband became a leper, if he engaged in a disgusting trade such as that of a tanner, if he ravished a virgin, or if he falsely accused her of pre-nuptial sin. The law of Jewish divorce goes back to Deuteronomy 24: 1. But the process of divorce remained on the whole exceedingly easy, and the problem was the interpretation of the law as it is in Deuteronomy 24: 1. There it is laid down that a man can divorce his wife if he finds in her some indecency. How was that phrase to be interpreted? There were in this matter two schools of thought. There was the School of Shammai. They interpreted the matter with utter strictness. A matter of indecency was adultery and adultery only. The other school was the School of Hittel. They interpreted that crucial phrase as widely as possible. To such a pass had things come that in the time of Jesus, women hesitated to marry at all because marriage was so insecure. When Jesus spoke as he did he was speaking on a subject, which was a burning issue, and He was breaking down barriers for women by seeking to restore marriage to the position it ought to have. The real essence of the passage is that Jesus insisted that the loose sexual morality of His day must be mended. Those who sought marriage only for pleasure must be reminded that marriage is also for responsibility. Those who regarded marriage simple as a means of gratifying their physical passions must be reminded that it was also a spiritual unity. Jesus was building a wall of protection and stability around the home, which they desperately needed at that time.

PRAYER

Let us pray. God of compassion and grace, in Your steadfast love accompany us here. Thank You for everything You have given us, as You always work to restore and renew Your people. Give us the grace to strengthen our marriage and the courage to overcome all the difficulties. Teach us to overcome bitterness with Your love, brokenness with Your life, and give us hope through the death and resurrection of Your Son, Jesus Christ our Lord. Amen

MT TABOR, FEAST DAY OF THE TRANSFIGURATION AUGUST 6TH

Matthew 17: 1-9 Jesus took Peter, James, and John his brother, and led them up a high mountain by themselves. And He was transfigured before them; his face shone like the sun and his clothes became white as light. And behold, Moses and Elijah appeared to them, conversing with him. Then Peter said to Jesus in reply, "Lord, it is good that we are here. If you wish, I will make three tents here, one for You, one for Moses, and one for Elijah." While he was still speaking, behold, a bright cloud cast a shadow over them, then from the cloud came a voice that said, "This is my beloved Son, with whom I am well pleased; listen to him." When the disciples heard this, they fell prostrated and were very much afraid. But Jesus came and touched them, saying, "Rise, and do not be afraid." And when the disciples raised their eyes, they saw no one else but Jesus alone. As they were coming down from the mountain, Jesus charged them, "Do not tell the vision to anyone until the Son of Man has been raised from the dead."

REFLECTIONS

We must remember that Jesus was just about to set out to Jerusalem
and to the cross. We have already looked at one great moment when
he asked his disciples who they believed Him to be, in order that
He might discover if anyone had realized who he was. But there was
one thing Jesus would never do, and that is he would never take any
step without the approval of God His Father. At this particular place
we see Jesus seeking and receiving approval from the Father. Are we
not all privileged just to be here, to stand here, and to pray here, and
yes, we too seek our heavenly Father's approval. What happened on
the Mt. of Transfiguration we can never know, but we do know that
something tremendous did happen. Jesus had gone there to seek
the approval of God for the decisive step he was about to take. It
was there that Moses and Elijah appeared to him. It was consistent
Jewish belief that Elijah was to be forerunner and herald of the

*Mt Tabor – Located above the Jezreel Valley, and not part of any mountain
range, Mount Tabor looks like a high mountain. Mt. Tabor is identified by
many theologians as the high mountain which Jesus climbed, followed by
Peter, James and John, where he was transfigured before them.*

Basilica of the Transfiguration – The first basilica upon the plateau of Mount Tabor in honor of the transfiguration of Jesus was built in the 4th Century. The present basilica was built by the Custody of the Holy Land in 1924. The Basilica has three naves divided by massive pillars and robust arcades and the chapel dedicated to Moses and Elijah.

Messiah, and it was also believed by at least some Jewish teachers that, when the Messiah came, Moses would accompany him. Moses was the great lawgiver of the people of Israel; Elijah was the greatest of the prophets. It was as if the princes of Israel's life and thought and religion told Jesus to go on. Not only did the greatest lawgiver and the greatest prophet assure Jesus that He was right; the very voice of God came telling him that He was on the right way. It was the experience on the Mount of Transfiguration, which enable Jesus to walk the way to the Cross. In one sentence it said of the three apostles, "When they were fully awake they saw His glory".

Transfiguration on Mt. Tabor.

In life we miss so much because our minds are asleep. There are certain things, which are liable to keep our minds closed or asleep. There is **prejudice**. We may be so set in our ideas that our minds are shut. A new idea knocks at the door, but we are like sleepers who will not awake. There is love of **ease**. There is a kind of defense mechanism in us that makes us automatically shut the door against any disturbing thoughts. A man may drug himself or drink too much until his mind is sound asleep, and he misses so much of life. I guess we all need to pray to God and ask Him to keep us awake to His word.

COMING DOWN FROM MT. TABOR

Mark 9: 14-29 As Jesus came down the mountain with Peter, James and John, and approached the disciples, they saw a large crowd standing around, and scribes in lively discussion with them. Immediately on catching sight of Jesus, the whole crowd was overcome with awe. They ran up to greet Him. He asked them, "What are you discussing among yourselves?" "Teacher," a man in the crowd replied, "I have brought my son to You because he is possessed by a mute spirit. Whenever it seizes him it throws him down; he foams at the mouth and grinds his teeth and becomes rigid. Just now I asked Your disciples to expel him, but they were unable to do so." He replied by saying to the crowd, "What an unbelieving lot you are! How long must I remain with you? How long can I endure you? Bring him to me." When they did so the spirit caught sight of Jesus and immediately threw the boy in convulsions. As he fell to the ground he began to roll around and foam at the mouth. Then Jesus questioned the father: "How long has this been happening to him?" "From childhood," the father replied. "Often it throws him into the fire and into water. You would think it would kill him. If out of the kindness of your heart you can do anything to help us, please do!" Jesus said, "If you can? Everything is possible to a man who trust." The boy's father immediately exclaimed, "I do believe! Help my lack of trust!" Jesus, on seeing a crowd rapidly gathering, reprimanded the unclean spirit by saying to him, "Mute and deaf spirit, I command you: Get out of him and never enter him again!" Shouting, and throwing the boy into convulsions, it came out of him; the boy became like a corpse, which caused many to say, "He is dead." But Jesus took him by the hand and helped him to his feet. When Jesus arrived at the house His disciples began to ask Him privately, "Why is it that we could not expel it?" He told them, "This kind you can drive out only by prayer."

Mt. Tabor – The main altar of the Basilica of the Transfiguration. Here Jesus was Transfigured before Peter, James and John and his garments became gistening, intensely white.

REFLECTION

"This is a good place for us to be", Peter said, but yet they too had to come down the mountain. It has been said that in any religion there must be solitude. The solitude is necessary, for a man must keep his contact with God, but if a man in his search for the essential solitude, shuts himself off from his fellow-men, shuts his ears to their appeal for help, shuts his heart to the cry of their tears, that is not religion.

Many a man can face a great disaster or a great loss with calm serenity and yet loses his temper if a meal is badly cooked or the children are loud. The amazing thing about Jesus was that He could serenely face the Cross, and just as calmly deal with the day-to-day emergencies of life. The reason was that He did not keep

God only for the crisis as so many of us do. He walked the daily paths of life with Him, and we should too.

Let us look how He was to meet this moment of despair. "Bring the boy to me", he said. It was as if Jesus said, " I do not know how I am ever to change these disciples of Mine, but I can at this moment help this boy. Let me get on with the present task, and not despair of the future." If we sit and think about the state of the world, we may well become very depressed. The surest way to avoid pessimism and despair is to take what immediate action we can, and there is always something to be done.

When the apostles were by themselves they asked the cause of their failure. What He said to them was in effect – "You don't live close enough to God". They had been equipped with power, but it needed prayer to maintain it. There is a deep lesson here for all of us.

God may have given us a gift, but unless we maintain close contact with Him it may wither and die. That is true of any gift. God may give a man great natural gifts as a priest, but unless he maintains contact with God, he may in the end become only a man of words and not a man of power and grace. God may give a man or woman a gift of music or of song, but unless he or she maintains contact with God, they may become a mere professional, who uses the gift only for gain, which is a dreary thing.

SONG

> Holy God, We Praise Thy Name
> Lord of all, we bow before Thee
> All on earth Thy scepter claim
> All in heav'n above adore Thee
> Infinite Thy vast domain
> Everlasting is Thy name!

Town of Nain

Luke 7: 11-17 Jesus was on his way to a town called Nain; and his disciples and a great crowd accompanied Him on the journey. When he came near the gate of the town he saw a man who had died was being carried out to burial. He was His mother's only son, and she was a widow. There was a great crowd of townspeople with her. When the Lord saw her He was moved to the depths of His heart for her and said to her, "Don't go on weeping!" He went up and touched the coffin. Those who were carrying it stood still. "Young man," He said, "I tell you rise! And the dead man sat up and began to speak. And He gave him back to his mother. And awe gripped them all. They glorified God saying, "A great prophet has been raised up amongst us," and "God has graciously visited His people." This story about him went out in all Judea and all the surrounding countryside.

Reflection

Jesus claim was for a man who had been marked for death. Jesus is not only the Lord of life, but He is the Lord of death who Himself triumphed over the grave, and who has promised that, because He lives, we too shall live if we follow Jesus. Jesus may use you to touch other people in a very positive way. Remember you may be the only light some people ever see.

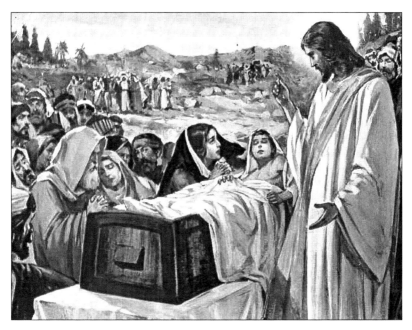

In the city of Naim Jesus raises the widow's son from the dead.

CHAPTER 9
TIBERIAS — SEA OF GALILEE
(Sea of Galilee, Capernaum, Mt. of Beatitude, Peter's Primacy, Loaves & Fishes,)

Sea of Galilee

Jesus Chooses His Disciples
Like 6: 12-19
Luke 5-: 1-11

Catching of the Fish-Temple Tax
Mark 4: 35-41

Jesus Calms the Storm
Matthew 14: 22-23

Jewish Tradition
Luke 13: 18-19

Mustard Seed Parable

Peter's Primacy
John 21: 1-15
Mark 1: 35-39 (Quiet Place Near the Sea)
Mark 6: 30-34

Loaves & Fishes
John 6: 1-13
Matthew 14: 1-12 (Jewish Custom & Law)

Capernaum
Shekel in the fish's mouth
Matthew 17: 24-27

Paralyzed Man in Peter's House
Mark 2: 1-12

Healing of Peter's Mother-in-law
Mark 1: 29-34

Jesus warns Chorazin & Bethsaida
Matthew 11: 20-24

Centurion's Servant
Matthew 8: 5-13

Much will be given and required
Mark 4: 21-25

Material Possessions in Life
Luke 12: 13-31

Who touched Me?
Mark 5: 30-34

Mt. of Beatitude
Matthew 5: 3-12

Swine Run into the Sea
Luke 8: 26-38

**Ten Reasons to Believe in a God
Who Allows Suffering**

Mt. Carmel
1 King 18: 20-39

Northern View Sea of Galilee – Taken from the Mt. of the
Beatitudes facing the northern part of the Sea of Galilee.

JESUS CHOOSES HIS MEN

Luke 6: 12-19 In these days Jesus went away into a mountain to pray; and He spent the whole night in prayer to God. When day came He called his disciples. From them He chose twelve, whom He also called apostles-Simon, whom he named Peter, and Andrew his brother, and James, and John, and Philip, and Bartholomew, and Matthew, and Thomas, and James the son of Alphaeus, and Simon who was called the Zealot, and Judas the son of James, and Judas Iscariot, who became a traitor. He came down with them and took His stand with them on a place in the plain; and there was a great crowd of His disciples there, and a great crowd of people from all Judea and Jerusalem and from the coastal district of Tyre and Sidon, who had come to listen to Him and to be healed from their diseases; and those who were distressed by unclean spirits were healed and the whole crowd sought to touch Him because power went out from Him, and He healed all.

Reflection

Here we see Jesus choosing His men. It is amazing that Jesus needed human friendship. They were very ordinary men. They were not wealthy, famous, or influential men, they had no special education and they were considered ordinary people. It is as if Jesus said, "Give Me twelve ordinary men and I will change the world." The work of Jesus is not in the hands of men who are called great, but in the hands of ordinary people like ourselves.

God never calls the equipped; He equips those who are called.

St. Theresa of Avila had said, "Christ has no body now on earth but yours, no feet but yours, you are the eyes through which he is to go about doing good."

Luke 5: 1-11 Jesus was standing on the shore of the Lake of Gennesaret while the crowds pressed in upon him to listen to the word of God. He saw two boats riding close to the shore; the fishermen had disembarked from them and were washing their nets. He embarked on one of the boats, which belonged to Simon, and asked him to push out a little from the land. He sat down and continued to teach the crowds from the boat. When He stopped speaking, He said to Simon, "Push out into the deep water and let down your nets for a catch." Simon answered, "Master, we have toiled all night long and we caught nothing, but if You say so, I will let down the nets." When they had done so they enclosed a great crowd of fishes and their nets were torn with the numbers so they signaled to their partners in the other boat to come and help them. They came and they filled both the boats so that they began to sink. When Simon Peter saw this he fell at Jesus' knees. "Leave me, Lord," he said, " because I am a sinful man." Wonder gripped him and all who were amazed with Him at the number of fishes they had caught. It was the same with James and John, Zebedee's sons, who were partners with Simon. Jesus said to Simon, "From now on you will be catching men." So they brought the boats to land and they left everything and followed Him.

COMMENTARY & REFLECTION

The famous sea of water in Galilee which is called by three names - Sea of Galilee, the Sea of Tiberias and the Lake of Gennesaret. Gennesaret is really the name of the lovely plain on the west side of the lake, a most fertile piece of land. There are several schools of thought on how Gennesaret got its name. From kinnor, which means a harp, either because its fruit is sweet as the sound of a harp, or because, the voice of its waves is pleasant as the voice of the harp. Here we are confronted with a turning point in the career of Jesus. Last time we heard him preach he was in the synagogue and now he is at the lakeside. The time has come where the door of the synagogue would be shut to him, and his church will be the lakeside, the open road, and his pulpit would be a boat. He would go anywhere where men would listen to Him.There are three conditions present for this miracle of catching fish to be possible:

1. There are the eyes that see. There is no need to think that Jesus created a school of fishes for this occasion. In the Sea of Galilee there were phenomenon like schools of fishes, which covered the sea as if it were solid for 100

The disciples follow Jesus' suggestion and catch many fish.

yards. Most likely Jesus' keen eye saw just such a school, and His keen sight made it look like a miracle. We need these eyes that really see. Many people saw steam raise the lid of a kettle; only James Watt went on to think of a steam engine. Many people saw an apple fall; only Isaac Newton went on to think out the law of gravity. The earth is full of miracles for the eyes that see. We all need to take time to see these miracles and sometime we need to point them out to each other. What you see may be a signal grace from God.

2. There is the spirit in us that will make an effort. If Jesus said it, tired as he was Peter, was prepared to try again. For most people the disaster of life is that they give up just one effort too soon. How true this is in our own lives.

3. There is the spirit, which will attempt what seems hopeless. The night had past, and time for fishing was over. All the circumstances were unfavorable, but Peter said, "Let circumstance be what they may, if you say so, Jesus we will try again." Too often we wait because the time is not right. If we wait for a perfect set of circumstances, we will never begin at all. If we truly want a miracle, we must take Jesus at His word when He asks us to attempt the impossible. These experiences we have enjoyed so far on this pilgrimage would never had been possible if you had not said yes to Jesus, and attempted this almost impossible task of traveling to the Holy Land. Yes, St. Peter let down his net into the troubled sea of this life, certain that sooner or later God will make him an instrument of salvation to many. Be patient with God because He's not done with you yet

THE STORM ON THE SEA OF GALILEE

Mark 4: 35-41 That day as evening drew on He said to them, "Let us cross over to the farther shore." Leaving the crowd, they took Him away in the boat in which He was sitting, while the other boats accompanied Him. It happened that a bad squall blew up. The waves were breaking over the boat and it began to ship water badly. Jesus was in the stern through it all, sound asleep on a cushion. They finally woke Him and said to Him, "Teacher, does it not matter to You that we are going to drown?" He awoke and

Sea of Galilee – Northern part the Sea of Galilee, Capernaum, Mt of Beatitudes, where the Multiplication of the Loaves and Fishes are all located.

rebuked the wind and said to the sea: "Quiet! Be still!" The wind fell off and everything grew calm. Then He said to them, "Why are you lacking in faith?" A great awe overcame them at this. They kept saying to one another, "Who can this be that the wind and the sea obey him?"

REFLECTION

The Sea of Galilee was notorious for its storms. These are caused by winds coming from the heights of Hauran, plateau of Trachonitis, and the summit of Mt. Hermon caught and compressed in such a way that, rushing with tremendous force through a narrow space and then being suddenly released, they agitate the Sea of Galilee. Interesting to note, the words Jesus addressed to the wind and the waves are exactly the same as he addressed to the demon-possessed man in Mark 1:25. Just as an evil demon possessed the man the people at that time thought so too, that the destructive power of the storm was also the evil power of the demons at work in the realm of nature.

To voyage with Jesus was to voyage in peace even in a storm. Jesus gives us peace in the storm of sorrow. When sorrow comes into our lives, He tells us of His glory in the life to come. He changes darkness into sunshine at the thought of life eternal.

He gives us peace in the storm of anxiety. The chief enemy of peace is worry, worry for ourselves, and worry about the unknown future, worry about those we love. But Jesus speaks to us of a Father whose hand will never cause His child a needless tear and of a love beyond which neither we nor those we love can ever drift.

He gives us peace when life's problems involve us in tension and uncertainty. There come times in everyone's lives when we do not know what to do, and when we stand at some cross-road in life, and do not know which way to take. If then we turn to Jesus and say to him, " Lord, what will you have me do? And the way will be clear. To ask His will and then to submit to it is the way to peace in our lives.

PETER WALKS ON THE SEA

Matthew 14: 22-23 Immediately afterward, while dismissing the crowds, Jesus insisted that His disciples get into the boat and precede him to the other side. When He had sent them away, he went up on the mountain by himself to pray, remaining there alone as evening drew on. Meanwhile the boat, already several hundred yards out from shore, was being tossed about in the waves raised by strong headwinds. At about three in the morning, he came walking toward them on the water and they were terrified. "It is a ghost!" They said, and in their fear they began to cry out. Jesus hastened to reassure them: "Get hold of yourself! It is I. Do

The apostles beg Jesus for help, and He, standing up, calms the storm.

not be afraid!" Peter spoke up and said, "Lord, if it is really you, tell me to come to you across the water." "Come!" he said. So Peter got out of the boat and began to walk on the water, moving toward Jesus. But when he perceived how strong the wind was, becoming frightened, he began to sink and cried out, "Lord, save me!" Jesus at once stretched out His hand and caught him. "How little faith you have! He exclaimed. "Why did you falter?" Once they had climbed into the boat, the wind died down. Those who were in the boat showed Him reverence, declaring, "beyond doubt You are the Son of God!"

Reflection

Peter was given to acting upon impulse and without thinking of what he was doing. It was his mistake that again and again he acted without fully facing the situation and without counting the cost. Peter's whole trouble was that he was ruled by his heart and, although he might sometimes fail, his heart was always in the right place and the instinct of his heart was always love. Because Peter acted on impulse, He often failed and came to grief. It was always Jesus' insistence that a man should look at all the situations and difficulties before making a decision. Jesus was completely honest with man; he always warned us of how difficult it would be to follow Him. A great deal of man's failure is due to acting upon an emotional moment without counting the cost. But Peter never finally failed, for always in the moment of his failure he clutched at Christ. The wonderful thing about him is that every time he fell, he rose again; even his failures brought him closer and closer to Jesus Christ. A saint is not a man who never fails; a saint is a man who gets up and goes on again every time he falls. We too can expect to fall in our life, but we pray that these temporary falls makes us love Jesus that much more.

Sea of Galilee – Fishing Boat on the Sea of Galilee

THERE ARE TWO SEAS
A Parable by Bruce Barton

There are two seas in Israel. One is fresh, and fish are in it. Splashes of green adorn its banks. . Trees spread their branches over it, and stretch out their thirsty roots to dip of its healing water. Along its shore the children play. The River Jordan makes this sea with sparkling water from the hills. So it laughs in the sunshine. And men build their houses near to it, and birds their nests, and every kind of life is happier because it is there.

The River Jordan flows on south into another sea. Here is no splash of fish, no fluttering leaf, no song of birds, no children laughter. Travelers choose another route, unless on urgent business. The air hangs above its water and neither man nor beast nor fowl will drink. What makes this mighty difference in these two neighboring seas? Not the River Jordan. It empties the same good water into both. Not the soil in which they lie, not the country round about. This is the difference. The Sea of Galilee receives, but does not keep the Jordan. For every drop that flows into it, another drop flows out. The giving

Jesus Walks on the Sea of Galilee

and receiving go on in equal measure. The other sea is shrewder, hoarding its income jealously. It will not be tempted into any generous impulse. Every drop it gets, it keeps. The Sea of Galilee gives and lives. This other sea gives nothing. It is named the Dead Sea.

There are two seas in Israel. There are two kinds of people in the world. Which kind are we?

SEA OF GALILEE REFLECTION-REACHING OUT
Fr. Frank P. DeSiano, C.S.P.

He invited me and I was afraid. I was only a simple fisherman, used to getting up early, staying up late, searching the lake endlessly for signs of fish. I got used to the strain and struggle of pulling in the net, the excitement and fatigue fused together. I got used to the quiet, peaceful monotony of sewing the torn net.

Sea of Galilee – This is the place where Christianity has its earliest origins.
Here Jesus gathered his disciples and performed most of his miracles.
This is truly the "Lake of Jesus."

Then He invited me. And everything has been different since then. He invited me to follow, along with my brother and friends, as we wandered the roads in Galilee. He astonished us by what He did. His teaching kept me, and the crowds around me, spellbound.

Then He shocked me. Because He invited me to go out myself, with my brothers, to announce His Kingdom in His name. To even bring his Kingdom by the exchange of peace, by the prayers we'd say, by the healings we would sometimes do.

I never thought I could do it. I stayed up all night worrying about what would happen. He had to encourage me. He reminded me that it was the hearts of people I now was fishing for:

I went on his invitation. I spoke His word to others. I acted as He acted. I shared what Jesus gave me to share, even to consoling, to freeing people from evil, to bringing God's healing to the broken.

He invited me. I was afraid, but after I said "yes," I began to realize what Jesus was all about - **THE INVITATION**.

You see we are all called and invited. This is evident by your mere presence on this trip. You see God will use you to touch other people if you only let him. He invited me. I was afraid, but after I said "yes," I began to realize what Jesus was all about - **THE INVITATION**.

PETER'S PRIMACY
AFTER THE RESURRECTION

John 21: 1-15 Jesus revealed Himself again to His disciples at the Sea of Tiberias. He revealed himself in this way. Together were Simon Peter, Thomas, and Nathaniel from Cana in Galilee, Zebedee's sons, and two others of his disciple. Simon Peter said to them, " I am going fishing," They said to him, " We also will come with you." So they went out and got into the boat, but that night they caught nothing. When it was already dawn, Jesus was standing on the shore; but the disciples did not realize that it was Jesus. Jesus said to them, "Children, have you caught anything to eat?" They answered Him, "No". So He said to them, "Cast the net over the right side of the boat and you will find something." So they cast it, and were not able to pull it in because of the number of fish. So the disciples whom Jesus loved said to Peter, "It is the Lord." When Simon Peter heard that it was the Lord, he tucked in his garment, for he was lightly clad, and jumped into the sea. The other disciples came in the boat, for they were not far from shore, only about a hundred yards, dragging the net with fish. When they climbed out on shore, they saw a charcoal fire with fish on it and bread. Jesus said to them, "Bring some of the fish you just caught. So Simon Peter went over and dragged the net ashore full of one hundred fifty-three large fish. Even though there were so many, the net was not torn. Jesus said to them, "Come, have breakfast." And none of the disciples dared to ask him, "Who are you"? because they realized it was the Lord.

Church of the Primacy – The church was built by the Franciscans in 1934 on the outline of an ancient edifice. The rock, called Mensa Christi, brings back the memory of the second miraculous draught of fish in the Sea after the resurrection and the primacy conferred by Jesus on Peter when He said to him: Feed my lambs ...Tend my sheep (John 21: 15-17).

Author standing on the rock inside this church.

Jesus came over and took the bread and gave it to them, and in like manner the fish. This was now the third time Jesus was revealed to his disciples after being raised from the dead.

Reflection

What we learn from here is that, on our own, we can do nothing, but with Jesus we can do many things (Phil 4: 12-13). They labored all the night and took nothing. Now they are under divine direction and a new power was loose. They dragged in a net containing 153 fish, and they counted them that day.

The Easter message means that, God can turn prostitutes like Mary Magdalen into disciples, broken reeds like Peter into rocks! Our God is the God of second chances.

Before He gives us strength He makes us feel our emptiness-come and eat at the table of friendship. Peter do you love Me more than these? Yes Lord! Therefore, Feed My sheep and lambs, which means please look after my weak sheep. Give them hope and encouragements. Let us not be discouraged by our weakness; let us keep steadfast in the Love of God. Let us leave the past to the mercy of God, the present to His love and the future to His Providence. Peter did not let his failings defeat him in spite of his weakness. We too are called to do the same and trust God. Christ says to you and me now. I have no hands, feet, would you lend me yours? Please give me yours?

Read in the Cave Near Peter's Primacy

See yourself sitting in a cave not far from the shore of the Sea of Galilee…Jesus comes to you and the two of you sit down together… Jesus looks upon you with great love and says…. Receive this love from Me.

Then Jesus blesses you: He places His hands on your **head** and says to you "Receive the **gifts of the mind.**

Jesus places His hands on your **ears**: and says, "**Receive the gift of listening clearly and with lov**e." Receive this gift….

Jesus places His hand on your **eyes**: and says, "**Receive the gift of seeing deeply.**" Again receive this gift.

Jesus place His hand on your **mouth**: and says, "**Receive the gift of speaking kindly and justly**". Receive this gift.

Jesus places His hand on your **heart**: "Receive **the gifts of compassion and forgiveness**." Receive this gift.

Jesus places His hands on your **feet: and says, "Receive the gift of going to those in need."** Receive this gift.

Then, Jesus holds your hands and says to you: These hands are made for both giving and receiving. He is looking into your eyes now and says to you: "The gifts that you have received, give as a gift."

(This is one of my favorite places looking down upon the Sea of Galilee very much like Jesus did during his time here. I always think about the one question I would ask Jesus if He was here. I just wished I could stop the clock, so as to absorb this beautiful view, these feelings of Jesus' presence, and this flow of God's grace that is coming upon us now.)

THE LOAVES AND FISHES

John 6: 1-13 After these things Jesus went away across the Sea of Galilee, that is, the Sea of Tiberias. A great crowd was following him, because they were watching the signs, which he did on those who were ill. Jesus went up into the hill and he was sitting there with His disciple. The Passover, the Feast of the Jews, was near. When Jesus lifted up his eyes and saw that a great crowd was coming to Him, He said to Philip: "Where are we to buy

Cave near Peter Primacy – Legend tells us that Jesus spent the night in this cave before he came forward to select his disciples. The cave is located near Peter's Primacy near the Sea of Galilee.

bread for these to eat?" He was testing Philip when He said this, for He himself knew what He was going to do. Philip answered Him: "Seven pounds worth of bread is not enough to give each of them a little to eat." One of the disciples said to Him, it was Andrew, Simon Peter's brother. "There is a boy here who has five barley loaves and two little fishes. But what use are they among so many?" Jesus said: "Make the men sit down." There was much grass in the place. So the men sat down to the number of about five thousand. So Jesus took the loaves and gave thanks for them, and dividing them up among those who were reclining there. So too He gave them of the fishes, as much as they wished. When they were satisfied, He said to the disciples: "Collect the broken pieces that are left over, so that nothing may be wasted." So they collected them, and they filled twelve baskets with the broken pieces of the loaves, which remained over after the people had eaten.

Church of the Multiplication of the Loaves and Fishes – A mosaic found in the Benedictine Church of the Multiplication of the Loaves and Fishes at Tabgha, traditional site of this miracle.

REFLECTION

We may view the multiplication of loaves and fishes as a simple miracle or it may be really a sacramental meal in disguise. The story represents the biggest miracle of all. One that changed not loaves and fishes, but men and woman. It was Andrew who said, "I'll see what I can do, and I'll trust Jesus to do the rest." It was Andrew who brought the boy to Jesus with the fish and barley loaves that made the miracle possible. No one ever knows what will come out of it when we bring someone to Jesus. If parents raise their children in the knowledge and love of God, no one can ever say what mighty things that a child may do for God, his fellow man and the church. We never know what possibilities we are releasing when we bring someone to Jesus. Jesus needs what we can bring Him. It may not be much but he needs it. The world may be denied miracle after miracle, because we will not bring to Jesus what we have and what we are. If only we open ourselves to the love of God, there is no saying what He could do with us and through us. God will use you to touch other people if you only let Him.

We may be sorry and embarrassed that we have little to bring and rightly so, but that is no reason for failing to bring what we have. Little is always much in the hands of Christ. God doesn't call us to do great things, but to do little things graciously.

QUIET PLACE NEAR SEA OF GALILEE

Mark 1: 35-39 Very early, when it was still night, Jesus rose and went out. He went away to a desert place and there He was praying. Simon and his friends tracked Him down and said to Him, "They are all searching for You," Jesus said to them, "Let us go somewhere else, to the nearby villages, that I may proclaim the good news there too, for that is why I came forth." So he went to their synagogues, all over Galilee, proclaiming the good news as he went, and casting out demons.

REFLECTION

Even Jesus realized that he couldn't continue his ministry unless he went back to the Father in private prayer. In prayer we give the perfect mind of God an opportunity to nourish our mental powers. Jesus realized that before He meets man, He must meet God. If prayer was necessary for Jesus, how much more must it be necessary for us? Prayer will never do our work, but what it will do is give us the strength for us to do the work that must be done. The dream of Jesus was a time when God's will would be done on earth as it is in heaven, and earth and heaven be one.

Mark 6: 30-34 The apostles returned to Jesus and reported to Him all that they had done and what they had taught. He said, to them, "Come by yourselves to an out of the way place and rest a little." People were coming and going in great numbers, making it impossible for them to so much as eat. So Jesus and the apostles went off in the boat by themselves to a deserted place. People saw them leaving, and many got to know about it. People from all the towns hastened on foot to the place, arriving ahead of them. Upon disembarking Jesus saw a vast crowd. He pitied them, for they were like a sheep without a shepherd; and He began to teach them at great length.

REFLECTION

One of the dangers of life is to be too constantly active. No one can work without rest, and no person can live a good Christian life unless they give themselves time with God. It may well be that the whole trouble in our lives is that we don't give God an opportunity to speak to us, because we do not know how to be still and to listen. We don't even give God a chance to recharge us with a spiritual strength and energy so necessary for our spiritual well being. How can we shoulder life's burden if we have no contact with Him, who is the Lord of all good life? How can we do God's work unless we have God's strength? A sheep without the shepherd cannot find the way. Left to ourselves we get lost in life, and it can be so bewildering. We can be standing at some cross-road in life and not know what way to take. It is only when Jesus leads, and we follow that we can truly find the way.

JEWISH CUSTOM & LAW

Matthew 14: 1-12 The Pharisees and scribes came to Jesus from Jerusalem and said, "Why do Your disciples break the tradition of the elders?" They do not wash (their) hands when they eat a meal."

He said to them in reply, "And why do you break the commandment of God for the sake of your tradition? For God said, "Honor your father and your mother, and whoever curses father or mother shall die." But you say, whoever says to father or mother, "Any support you might have had from me is dedicated to God," need not honor his father. You have nullified the word of God for the sake of your tradition. Hypocrites, well did Isaiah prophesy about you when He said: This people honors Me with their lips, but their hearts are far from Me; in vain do they worship Me, teaching as doctrines human precepts." He summoned the crowd and said to them, "Hear and understand. It is not what enters one's month that defiles that person, but what comes out of the mouth is what defiles one.

COMMENTARY ABOUT WHAT IS CLEAN AND UNCLEAN

This particular reading represents a head on clash between Jesus and the leaders of orthodox Jewish religion. It is something far more; it is a collision of two views of religion and two views of the demands of God. We must be quite clear that his idea of cleanness and uncleanness has nothing to do with physical cleanness, or, except distantly, with hygiene for its leaders. It is entirely a ceremonial matter. For a man to be clean was for him to be in a state where he might worship and approach God, and for him to be unclean was for him to be in a state where such an approach was impossible. This uncleanness was contracted by contact with certain persons or things. For instance, a woman was unclean if she had a hemorrhage, even if that hemorrhage was her normal monthly period. She was unclean for a stated time after she had had a child. Even dead bodies were considered unclean, and to touch it was to become unclean. Gentiles were also considered unclean. This uncleanness was transferable; it was so to speak, infectious. For instance, if a mouse touched a cooking pot, that pot was unclean and unless it was ritually washed and cleaned, everything put into it was unclean, and in turn anyone who touched the person who had so become unclean also became unclean.

This is not only a Jewish idea, it occurs in other religions. To a high-caste Indian anyone not belonging to his own caste is unclean and if that person becomes a Christian, he is still more seriously unclean.

The laws of cleanness and uncleanness have a further wide area of application. They laid down what a man might eat, and what he might not eat. Broadly speaking all fruit and vegetables were clean. But, in regard to living creatures, the laws were strict. These laws are found in Leviticus 11.

Many people have asked me to explain them on my trips and many guides will avoid talking about it. Let me try to briefly summarize them. Of beasts only those can be eaten who have part the cloven hoof and chew a cud. That is why no Jew can eat the flesh of the pig, the rabbit, or the hare. In no case may the flesh of an animal which has died a natural death be eaten (Deuteronomy 14: 21). In all cases the blood must be drained from the carcass; the orthodox Jew still buys his meat from a kosher butcher, who sells only meat so treated. Ordinary fat upon the flesh might be eaten, but the fat on the kidneys and on the entrails of the abdomen, which we call suet, might not be eaten. In regard to seafood, only sea creatures, which have both fins and scales, may be eaten. This means that shell fish such as lobsters and cat fish are unclean. All insects are unclean, with one exception, locusts. In the case of animals and fish there is a standard test, as we have seen, of what might be eaten, and what might not be eaten. In the case of birds there is no such test; and the list of unclean and forbidden birds is in Leviticus 11: 13-21.

There were certain identifiable reasons for all this. The refusal to touch dead bodies, or to eat the flesh of an animal which has died from natural causes, may well have had something to do with the belief in evil spirits. It would be easy to think of a demon as taking up residence in such a body, and so gaining entry into the body of the eater. This is a natural thought, for as blood flows away, life ebbs away. And the life belongs to God, and to God alone. The same idea explains the prohibition of eating the fat. The fat is the richest part of the carcass, and the richest part must be given to God. In some cases, although they are few, there was sound sense behind the prohibitions and the food laws.

The book <u>The Bible and Modern Medicine</u>, by Dr. Rendle Short points how many of these regulations were in fact wise from the point of view of health and hygiene. Dr. Short writes: "True, we eat the pig, the rabbit and the hare, but these animals are liable to parasitic infections and are safe only if the food is well-cooked. The pig is an unclean feeder, and harbors two worms, trichina and a tapeworm, which may be passed on to man. The danger is minimal under present conditions in this country, but it would have been far otherwise in Israel of old, and such food was better avoided." The prohibition of eating anything with blood in it comes from the fact that the blood is the life in Jewish thought.

These things would not in themselves matter very much, but the trouble and the tragedy were that they had become to the Scribes and Pharisees matters of life and death. To serve God, to be religious, was to observe these good laws. If we put it in the following way, we will see the result. To the Pharisaic mind, the prohibition of eating rabbit's or pig's flesh was just as much a commandment of God as the prohibition of adultery, and it was therefore just as much a sin to eat pork or rabbit as to seduce a woman and enjoy illegal sexual intercourse. Religion had got itself mixed up with all kinds of external rules and regulations and since it is much easier both to observe rules and regulation and to check up on those who do not, and these rules and regulations had become a religion to the Orthodox Jews. And that's the story behind the rules and regulations.

CAPERNAUM AREA

Introduction: The Temple in Capernaum was a very costly place to run. There were the morning and evening sacrifices each of which involved the offering of a year-old lamb. Along with the lamb were offered wine, flour and oil. The incense that was burned every day had to be bought and prepared. The costly hangings and the robes of the priests constantly wore out, and the robes of the High Priest were extremely expensive. All these expenses required money and it was for these reason and few more that they had a Temple Tax.

CAPERNAUM

Mark 2:1-12 He came back to Capernaum after a lapse of several days and word got around that He was at home. At that they began to gather in great numbers. There was no longer any room for them, even around the door. While He was delivering God's word to them, some people arrived bringing a paralyzed man to him. The four who carried him were unable to bring him to Jesus because of the crowd, so they began to open up the roof over the spot where Jesus was. When they had made a hole, they let down the mat on which the paralytic was lying. When Jesus saw their faith, He said to the paralyzed man, "My son, your sins are forgiven." Now some of the scribes were sitting there asking themselves: Why does the Man talk in that way? He commits blasphemy! Who can forgive sins except God alone?" Jesus was immediately aware of their reasoning, though they kept it to themselves, and He said to them: "why do you harbor these thoughts?" Which is easier, to say to the

paralytic, "Your sins are forgiven, or to say, stand up, pick up your mat and walk again." That you may know that the Son of Man has authority on earth to forgive sins," (He said to the paralyzed man) "I command you: Stand up! Pick up your mat and go home." The man stood and picked up his mat and went outside in the sight of everyone. They were awestruck; all gave praise to God saying," We have never seen anything like this!"

REFLECTION

We have to remember that sin and suffering were closely connected in the time of Christ. It was implicitly believed that if a man was suffering he had sinned. That is why Jesus began by telling the man that his sins were forgiven. Without that the man would never believe that he could be cured. They believed the man was ill because he had sinned, and if he was cured that was proof that his sins were forgiven, and no one could dispute this miracle. Also Christ forgave the man his sins first and cured the man second, because many times our spiritual life is much more important than our physical life. Ambush theology is the belief that there is a vengeful God out there just waiting for us to fall so that he can punish us. Many of us believe this even today. This is exactly the opposite what Jesus teaches us about His Father. Jesus taught us about a God of love, compassion and mercy.

Prayer: *My Lord God, I have no ideal where I am going, I do not see the road ahead of me, I cannot know for certain where it will end. Nor do I really know myself, and the fact that I think I am following your will does not mean that I am actually doing so. But I believe that the desire to please you does in fact please you. And I hope I have that desire in all that I am doing. I hope that I will never do anything apart from that desire. And I know that if I do this you will lead me by the right road, though I may know* *nothing about it. Therefore, I will trust you always, though I may seem to be lost and in the shadow of death. I will not fear, for you are ever with me, and you will never leave me to face my perils alone.* **Thomas Merton**

John 6: 35-71   Jesus said to them, " I am the bread of life; whoever comes to me will never hunger, and whoever believes in me will never thirst.   But I told you that although you have seen me you do not believe. Everything that the Father gives me will come to me, and I will not reject anyone who comes to me, because I came down from heaven not to do my own will but the will of the one who sent me. And this is the will of the one who sent me, that I should not lose anything of what he gave me, but that I should raise it on the last day. For this is the will of my Father, that everyone who sees the Son and believes in him may have eternal life, and I shall raise him on the last day.   The Jews murmured about him because he said, " I am the bread that came down from heaven, and they said, " Is this not Jesus, son of Joseph? Do we not know his father and mother?" Then how can he say, I have come down from heaven? Jesus answered and said to them, " No one can come to me unless the Father who sent me draw him, and I will raise him on the last day. It is written in the prophets: They shall all be taught by God. Everyone who listens to my Father and learns from him comes to me. Not that anyone has seen the Father except the one who is from God; he has seen the Father. Amen, amen, I say to you, whoever believes has eternal life. I am the bread of life. Your ancestors ate the manna in the desert, but they died; this the bread that comes down from heaven so that one may eat it and not die. I am the living bread that came down from heaven; whoever eats this bread will live forever; and the bread that I will give is my flesh for the life of the world." The Jews quarreled among themselves saying, "How can

Capernaum Synagogue – The synagogue a sumptuous structure of light colored limestone in a region in which the earth is black basaltic rock. These are the ruins of the place most frequently mentioned in the Gospels. Miracles such as the healing of Peter's mother-in-law, catching the fish with the silver shekel for the Temple Tax, and many others are mentioned as occurring here, and because of these, Capernaum is called the "City of Jesus".

this man give us flesh to eat?" Jesus said to them, Amen, amen, I say to you, unless you eat the flesh of the Son of Man and drink his blood, you do not have life within you. Whoever eats my flesh and drinks my blood has eternal life, and I will raise him on the last day. For my flesh is true food, and my blood is true drink. Whoever eats my flesh and drinks my blood remains in me and I in him. Just as the living Father sent me and I have life because of the Father, so also the one who feeds on me will have life because of me. This is the bread that came down from heaven. Unlike your ancestors who ate and still died, whoever eats this bread will live forever." These things he said while teaching in the synagogue in Capernaum.

Reflection

Here we see the Jews confirming the fact that Jesus was a carpenter's son and they had seen him grow up in Nazareth. They were unable to understand how one who was a tradesman and who came from a poor home could possibly be a special messenger from God. We must be very careful never to neglect a message from God because we despise or do not care for the messenger. God has many messengers, but the greatest of all was his son Jesus a Galilean carpenter. If you were to take a Neil Gallop poll at this moment in history you would find that Jesus was one of the most popular persons in the Galilean and Judean area at this time. As soon as He made this statement about Him being the bread that came down from heaven and whoever eats My flesh and drinks My blood remains in Me and I in him, his popularity drops. Even today many Catholics have a hard time understanding the true presence of Christ in the Blessed Sacrament. Was Jesus just going to remain with us in his words only (bible), or was he going to remain with us as God made man in the Blessed Sacrament? Each time an ordained priest says Mass, we have an opportunity to receive Jesus as the true bread that came down from heaven. It's awesome to think about that this promise Jesus gave us, was said here in this synagogue at Capernaum.

Peter's House Capernaum
Mother-in-Law Cured

Mark 1: 29-34 On leaving the synagogue He entered the house of Simon and Andrew with James and John. Simon's mother-in-law was lying sick with a fever. They immediately told Him about her. He approached, grasped her hand, and helped her up. The fever left her and she waited on them. When it was evening, after sunset, they brought to Him all who were ill or possessed by demons. The

Good Centurion appealing to Jesus to cure his servant.

whole town was gathered at the door. He cured many who were sick with various diseases, and He drove out many demons, not permitting them to speak because they knew Him.

REFLECTION

Jesus had come from the synagogue and had just entered Peter's house. This miracle tells us much about Jesus, and not much about the woman he cured. Jesus was never too tired to help and the demands of human need never came to Him as an intolerable nuisance. Jesus was not one of these people who are at their best in public and at their worst in private. No situation was too humble for him to help. This miracle tells us something about the woman who Jesus healed. No sooner had he healed her than she busied herself in attending to his needs and to the needs of the other guests. Peter's mother-in-law used

Author standing next to Peter's House in Capernaum.

the gift of her restored health to serve Jesus and to serve others. This is the way in which we should use every gift of God.

CHORAZIN & BETHSAIDA

Matthew 11: 20-24 Then He began to reproach the towns where most of His mighty deeds had been done, since they had not repented. "Woe to you, Chorazin! Woe to you, Bethsaida! For if the mighty deeds done in your midst had been done in Tyre and Sidon, they would long ago have repented in sackcloth and ashes. But I tell you; it will be more tolerable for Tyre and Sidon on the Day of Judgment than for you. And as for you, Capernaum: Will you be exalted to heaven? You will go down to the Netherworld. For if the mighty deeds done in your midst had been done in Sodom, it would have remained until this day. But I tell you it will be more tolerable for the land of Sodom on the Day of Judgment than for you."

REFLECTION

Chorazin was probably a town an hour journey north of Capernaum, and Bethsaida was a fishing village on the west bank of the Jordan River, just as the river entered the northern end of the Sea of Galilee. Clearly the most tremendous things happened in these towns, and yet we have no account of them whatever. We cannot condemn a man who never had the chance to know any better, but if a man who has had every chance to know the right does the wrong, then he does stand condemned. The greater our privileges have been, the greater is our condemnation if we fail to shoulder the responsibilities and accept the obligations, which these privileges bring with them. It was the sin of indifference. These cities did not attack Jesus, and they did not drive Him from their towns nor did they seek to crucify him, but they simply disregarded Him. Neglect can kill as much as persecution can. Indifference does not burn a religion to death; it freezes it to death. It does not behead it: it slowly suffocates the life out of it. We are faced with an interesting question. Is it a sin to do nothing? There are sins of action, sins of deed: but there is also a sin of inaction, and of absence of deeds. The real sin of Chorazin, of Bethsaida, and of Capernaum was the sin of doing nothing or the sin of omission. Do you think that if you were put on trial, they would have enough evidence to convict you of being a Christian?

Matthew 8:5-13 When Jesus had come into Capernaum, a centurion came to him. " Lord," he appealed to him, "my servant lies at home, paralyzed, suffering terribly." He said to him: "Am I to come and cure him?" "Lord", answered the centurion, "I am not worthy that you should enter my house, but only speak a word, and my servant will be cured. For even I am a man under authority, and I have soldiers under me. I say to one soldier, go! And he goes, and to another, do this! And he does it." Jesus was amazed when he heard this, and said to those who were following him, "This is the truth I tell you not even in Israel have I found so great a faith. I tell you that many will come from the east and west and will sit down at table with Abraham, Isaac and Jacob in the Kingdom of Heaven, but the sons of the Kingdom will be cast into outer darkness. There will be weeping and gnashing of teeth there." And Jesus said to the centurion, "Go let it be done for you as you have believed." And his servant was healed at that hour.

Reflection

These centurions were the long service regular soldiers of the Roman army. They were responsible for the discipline of the regiment, and they were the cement, which held the army together. We can say that the centurions were the finest men in the Roman army. It may well be that it was this centurion's unusual gentleness and love which so moved Jesus when they first met. Love always covers a multitude of sins, and the man who cares for his fellow man is always near Jesus Christ. If only we could have the faith of this centurion we too could receive the blessings of God. How many good things could enter our lives if we just take time to ask God for help? As we leave Capernaum let us all remember that many of the crosses we carry each day would be much lighter if we only ask God for His assistance.

The Synagogue in Capernaum

Matthew 17:24-27 When they came to Capernaum those who received the half shekel Temple tax came to Peter and said, " Does your teacher not pay the tax?" Peter said, " He does pay it." When he had gone into the house, before he could speak, Jesus said to him, "What do you think, Simon? From whom do earthly kings

*Peter extracts the half-shekel
from the fish, which Jesus
told him would be there.*

take tax and tribute? From their sons or from strangers? " When he
said, " From strangers," Jesus said to him, " So then the sons are
free, but so as not to set a stumbling block in anyone's way, go to
the sea, and cast a hook into it, and take the first fish which comes
up, and when you have opened its mouth, you will find a shekel.
Take it and give it to them for Me and for you."

REFLECTION

We may sometimes be inclined to take certain exemptions in life,
which will set a bad example to others. We must not only do our
duty, we must go beyond duty in order that we may show others
what they ought to do. This gospel tells any Christian especially the

Jewish Christian that, however unpleasant they might be, the duties of a citizen must be shouldered. It tells us that Christian and good citizenship go hand in hand. The person who exempts himself from the duties of a good citizen is not only failing in his citizenship, but is also failing in his religion.

Mark 4: 21-25 Jesus said to the crowd: "Is a lamp acquired to be put under a bushel basket or hidden under a bed? Is it not meant to be put on a stand? Things are hidden only to be revealed at a later time; they are covered so as to be brought out into the open. Let him who has ears to hear me, hear!" He said to them another time: "Listen carefully to what you hear. In the measure you give you shall receive, and more besides. To those who have, more will be given; from those who have not, what little they have will be taken away."

REFLECTION

What a man gets in his life is usually determined by his giving. One of the great facts of life is that we see our own reflection in other people. If we are cross, irritable and bad tempered, we will probably find other people equally unpleasant. If we wish others to love us, we must first love them. The man who would like friends must show himself friendly. It was because Jesus believed in men that men believed in Him. The more a person knows the more they are capable of knowing. The more knowledge a person has the more they can acquire. The more physical strength a man has, the more, within the limits of his bodily frame, he can acquire. The more a person trains, the more your body will be able to do. The more a person develops the skill of his hand, or eye, or mind, the more he is able to develop it. The more responsibility a man shoulders the more he can shoulder; the more decisions he compels himself to take, the better he is able to take them.

THE PLACE OF MATERIAL POSSESSIONS IN LIFE

Luke 12: 13-31 Someone in the crowd said to Jesus, "Teacher, tell my brother to give me my share of our inheritance." He replied, "Friend, who has set me up as your judge or arbiter?" Then He said to the crowd, "avoid greed in all its forms. A man may be wealthy, but his possessions do not guarantee him life."

He told them a parable in these words: " There was a rich man who had a good harvest. "What shall I do, he asked himself. "I have no place to store my harvest. I know, he said. "I will pull down my grain bins and build larger ones. All my grain and my goods will go there. Then I will say to myself: You have blessings in reserve for years to come. Relax! Eat heartily, drink well, and enjoy yourself." "But God said to him, "You fool! This very night your life shall be required of you. To whom will all this piled up wealth of yours go."? That is the way it works with the man who grows rich for himself instead of growing rich in the sight of God."

REFLECTION

In Palestine wealth was often in the form of costly raiment; the moths could get at the fine clothes and leave them ruined. But if a man clothes his soul with the garments of honor and purity and goodness, nothing on earth can injure them. If a man or woman seeks the treasures of heaven, his/her heart will be fixed on heaven; but if they seek the treasures of earth, then they will always be disappointed. Someday they will have to say good-bye to these earthly possessions, and realize that none of these possessions come to your spiritual aid. It's not the money that matters, but **how** and **who** we spend the money on that really counts. Use your money

wisely to bring good things to others, and there you will find peace.
Reach out and touch someone in a very positive way. You still have
time.

Mark 5: 30-34 Jesus was well aware of Himself that the power,
which issued from Him had gone out of Him; and immediately, in
the middle of the crowd, He turned and said: "Who touched My
clothes?" The disciples said to Him: "Look at the crowd that are
crushing You on every side, and what's the point of saying, "Who
touched me?" He kept looking all round to see who had done this.
The woman was terrified and trembling. She knew well what had
happened to her. She came and threw herself down before Him,
and told Him the whole truth. "Daughter!" He said to her, "Your
faith has cured you! Go, and be in good health, free from the
trouble that was your scourge."

*Mount of the Beatitude. Somewhere on this mountain Jesus gave the
Sermon on the Mount, of which the Beatitudes are the essence.*

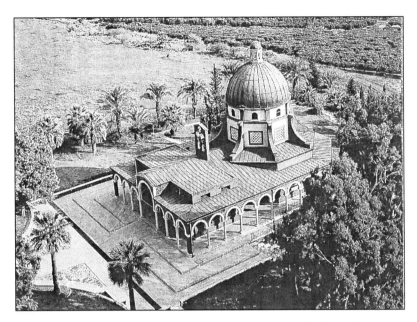

*Church of the Beatitudes – The church was built in 1938 by the architect
Barluzzi and is a lovely neo-Byzantine building in whose dome there are
eight stained-glass windows depicting the Beatitudes.*

REFLECTIONS

We will never produce anything great in life, unless we are prepared
to put something of ourselves, of our very life, of our very soul into
it. This is the cost of helping people. If we are ever to help our
fellow man, we must be ready to spend ourselves. Jesus was prepared
to pay the price of helping others, by getting involved with other
people. Just remember that once we go out to help this person and
that person, we too will experience this draining affect from us. We
must remember that once these good deeds are done, we have to go
back to the source of our energy and become filled up again. This
source of energy is God and the way we get our energy from God
is through prayer.

Matthew 5: 3-12

"Blessed are the poor in spirit, for theirs is the kingdom of
heaven.

Blessed are those who mourn, for they shall be comforted.

Blessed are the meek, for they shall inherit the earth.

Blessed are those who hunger and thirst for righteousness, for
they shall be satisfied.

Blessed are the merciful, for they shall obtain mercy.

Blessed are the pure in heart, for they shall see God.

Blessed are the peacemakers, for they shall be called sons of God.

Blessed are those who are persecuted for righteousness' sake,
for theirs is the kingdom of heaven.

Blessed are you when men revile you and persecute you and
utter all kinds of evil against you falsely on my account.
Rejoice and be glad, for your reward is great in heaven, for
so men persecuted the prophets who were before you.

READ AT MT. OF BEATITUDE
AFTER COMMUNION
Taken from "My Other Self", by Clarence Enzler

My dear friend, I am overjoyed to see you. I am with you, speaking
to you and listening to you. Realize that I am truly present. I am
within your soul. Close your ears and eyes to all distractions. Retire
within yourself, think My thoughts, and be with Me alone.

Do not be afraid. I am your God, your King, robed in majesty,
clothed with all the power. But I am also human, even as You. I
am your Saviour.

Do you note what I call you? My friend. Not my creature,
not My servant, but My friend. Yes, even more than that, you are
my brother, My sister, My mother. Whoever does the will of My

Father in heaven is My brother, My sister, My mother. I am glad you desire to watch a while with Me, to confide in Me and allow Me to confide in you.

Have you ever wondered what I would have said to you if you had been at My side as Peter was, and John, Mary, Martha, and the rest? Do you feel that they were especially favored to have lived when they did, because they saw Me, heard Me, touched Me? Yes, they were favored. But so are you. It is better for you to live now than at any other time in human history.

Do you not realize that this is My hour just as much as nineteen centuries ago? I see you just as clearly as I saw them. I love you as I loved them. I speak to you. Your good impulses, what are they but My words, My grace, the urgings of the Holy Spirit.

But still you are thinking: They saw You face to face. What was it that My disciples saw? They saw a man; a worker of wonders, yes, but only a man. It was many months before they knew Me as "He who is to come" – the Messiah, and as "He Who Is"- God. And when they knew Me at last it was not by the sight of their eyes but by faith. It could not be otherwise. No mortal can see God face to face and live on in this world. That is exactly how you know Me today: by faith.

Blessed are you because you see Me with surer eyes than those of your human nature: the eyes of faith. Blessed are you because you speak with Me in words more easily understood than those of your mouth: prayer of the heart. Yes, blessed are you, My friend, because you can more easily become intimately associated with Me than could My closest followers before the Last Supper.

Peter and Andrew, James, and John, and even My own Mother, for many years of their lives did not enjoy the wondrous privilege that awaits you every day. Never during those many months before the Supper did I unite Myself with them so closely as I am united with you in Holy Communion. Already you have had more moments of intimate union with Me in My sacrament than some of My dearest disciples had in their whole lives.

If you but let Me I will come to you daily in the Sacrament of Love. I will come as man, And I will come as God, bringing the Trinity most intimately into your soul. I do not stay away from you; it is you who stay away from Me.

Adam and Eve wished to be as God, and could not. But you, despite all your unworthiness can become "as God" daily in Holy Communion. I enter into you, live in you, and transform you. And when My Father looks on you, He sees you no longer, but Me, His only-begotten Son.

Indeed you are especially favored, far more than you can realize. Think how many there are in the world that do not even know My Name! Why are you so blessed and not these others? Why is it My will that you should be so intimate with Me? Why have I destined you from eternity for this happy hour with Me? Why have I sought you, called you, urged you, aided you all the days of your life to bring you close to Me?

It is because My love for you passes human understanding.

Do you wonder how you shall thank your God? Thank Me by making your soul a true home for Me, and from that home offering Myself and yourself in divine thanksgiving to the Holy and Undivided Trinity.

Think of this now. Think of it often. Think of it calmly, peacefully, and give Me your heart, your mind, your will. Say to My Father, "**I thank You, Lord, with all of myself. I will contemplate all Your wondrous deeds. I will be glad and rejoice, and I will sing praise to Your holy Name.**" Amen

Mustard Seed

Luke 13: 18,19 So Jesus said to them, "To what is the kingdom of God like, and to what will I compare it? It is like a grain of mustard seed, which a man took and cast into his garden, and it grew until it became a tree, and the birds of the air found a lodging in its branches."

Reflection

The important point in this parable is that the Kingdom of God will grow into a vast empire in which all kinds of people and nations will come together and will find the shelter and protection of God. We can safely say that there is room in the kingdom of God for a variety of traditions and cultures. To think ourselves right and everyone else wrong can lead to nothing but bitterness and strife. There is room in the Kingdom of God for a wide variety of experiences. One person may have a sudden changing of the heart (metanoia) and be able to tell you the day and hour and even the minute when this happened. Another person's heart may be open to Christ naturally and without crisis. Both experiences come from God. There is room in the Kingdom of God for a wide variety of ways of worship. In the more than 1600 denominations of Christianity we have more in common with each other than we do in differences. There is room in the kingdom for all nations under God. The mustard seed is indeed a symbol for us all. Our spiritual growth may take time, but will definitely lead us to heaven.

SWINE RUN INTO THE SEA — KURSI

Luke: 8: 26-38 Then they sailed to the territory of the Gerasenes, which is opposite Galilee. When He came ashore a man from the town, who was possessed by demons met Him. For a long time he had not worn clothes, he did not live in a house, but lived among the tombs. When he saw Jesus, he cried out and fell down before him, in a loud voice he shouted, "What have you to do with me, Jesus, son of the most High God? I beg you, do not torment me!" For he had ordered the unclean spirit to come out of the man. (It had taken hold of him many times, and he used to be bound with chains and shackles as a restraint, but he would break his bonds and be driven by the demon into deserted places.) Then Jesus asked him, "What is your name?" He replied, "Legion," because many demons had entered him. And they pleaded with Him not to order them to depart to the abyss. A herd of many swine was feeding there on the hillside, and they pleaded with him to allow them to enter those swine; and He let them. The demons came out of the man and entered the swine and the herd rushed down the steep bank into the lake and all were drowned. When the swineherds saw what had happened they ran away and reported the incident in the town and throughout the countryside. People came out to see what had happened, and when they approached Jesus, they discovered the man from whom the demons had come out sitting at his feet. He was clothed and in his right mind, and they were seized with fear. Those who witnessed it told them how the possessed man had been saved. The entire population of the region asked Jesus to leave them because they were seized with great fear.

REFLECTION

We could never compare the value of a herd of swine with the value of a man's immortal soul. The supreme tragedy of this story lies in its conclusion. Those who were herding the pigs ran back to the town and told what had happened, and the result was the people of the town asked Jesus to leave their territory at once. Here is human selfishness at its worst. It did not matter to these people that a man had been given back their reason, and all that mattered to them was that their pigs had perished. It is so often the case that people in effect say: I don't care what happens to anyone else, if my profits and my comfort and my ease are preserved. We must have a care that we too do not resent any helping of others, which reduces our own privileges.

Moses and Suffering & How it relates to us.
Nothing has changed.

SUFFERING-WHY?

Scripture states there were ten plagues that God imposed on the Egyptians before the Pharaoh released the Israelites from slavery, and there were Ten Commandments that God gave Moses. Somewhere in my life experiences I have heard it said that we should believe in a God who allows suffering. I have even read at some point in time a list of 10 reasons to believe in this and I also thought I would limit it to 10 reason since this books also discusses the 10 best areas to visit in Israel. Ten must be a lucky number so lets give it a try.

There is even an Apostolate of Suffering set up shortly after the Apparition at Fatima that supports the same belief. I thought it would be appropriate to reflect on these ten reasons as I can best recall them and show how they can relate to both to the Book of Exodus and our current life style.

Suffering will come to all of us at some point in our lives. For some it may be minor in nature and only temporary, and for others it may be permanent and life threatening. Moses experienced his suffering in the desert after leading the Israelites out of Egypt. He also experienced to some degree interior suffering, knowing that he would not be permitted to lead his people into the Promise Land. In our own spiritual life, we can lead some people only so far, and then someone else has to lead them further on their spiritual journey. Many times I have heard some people say that we all have to carry our crosses in life. I think, to some degree that these crosses have the potential to correct us, release us or prevent us from a life of sin. Others cross are redemptive, and still others may lead to our own repentance. We also try to understand which crosses come from God, and which ones come from our neighbors, friends, and family. There even are crosses, which come from within ourselves. I have always wondered why some people gracefully bear great sufferings; whereas, others get upset even at the smallest troubles. I believe that some people have learned about suffering while others have not. They have learned about it only by experiencing it. They have carried their crosses and suffered with them.

Rabbi Harold Kushner wrote a book called "When Bad Things Happen To Good People". He says that God does not respond to serious illness or other bad things by eliminating them or making them happen to people the world might think should suffer. God's response is to give strength and perseverance to overcome calamity and to summon friends and neighbors to ease the burden. Deetrick Bonhoffer had an interesting comment on suffering. He said, "Not only action but suffering is a way to freedom. In suffering, the deliverance consists in our being allowed to put the matter out of our own hands into God's hands".

TEN REASONS WHY TO BELIEVE IN A GOD WHO ALLOWS SUFFERING

1. **Suffering comes with freedom of choice and there is no way around this factor.** Loving parents long to protect their children from unnecessary pain. Moses mother tried to protect her son from being killed. Wise parents know the danger of over protection. The freedom to choose is at the heart of what are means to be human, and a world without choice would be worse than a world without pain. Worse yet would be people who could make wrong choices without feeling any pain and yet populate a world. No one is more dangerous than the liar, thief, or killer who doesn't feel the harm he is doing to himself and to others. Pharaoh used the Israelites for his own gain thus enslaving them for many years. His free choice resulted in suffering for many others as well as himself. God has given us a free will to choose. Love is based on that freedom.

2. **Pain can warn us of danger. I think we all hate pain, especially when we see it manifest itself in those we love.** Moses experiences this pain and was torn by it. The action he took was a result of the pain he felt for his countrymen. Pain and pleasure are the two biggest motivators in this world, but pain is the greater. Leprosy can cause deformity as well as blindness and the loss of fingers and toes. Leprosy causes you to lose feeling in your hands and feet. In India the rats would find which patients had feeling and which ones did not. The rats would come in at night and start to bite the patients. If

a patient moved, the rat would run, if not they would eat half the finger overnight and the patient would feel nothing. Pain helps us by warning us of danger. We have a built in safety device to warn us of danger. We have a God who built this in us for a reason, and it can't be turned off. We pray that we all lose the Leprosy in our own heart (lack of feeling for our fellow man). The bite of a rat is one thing, but the bite of sin is even more sorrowful. Moses had to learn for himself the consequences of sin and he felt it.

3. **I think that suffering takes us to the edge of eternity**. If death is the end of everything, then a life filled with suffering isn't fair. But if the end of this life brings us to the threshold of eternity, then the most fortunate people in the universe are those who discover, through suffering, that this life is not all we have to live for. Those who find themselves and God through suffering have not wasted their pain. The whole book of Exodus is about suffering and in the end how the Israelites found God. The fact that there is a God who cares for them and understood their suffering, gave them a sign of hope.

4. **Suffering can reveal what is in our hearts.** Suffering often occurs at the hand of others, as was the case with the Israelites. But it has a way of revealing what is in our own hearts. Remember, it is not the problems in life that matter, but how we react to the problems. Strength and weakness of heart is found not when everything is going our way, but when suffering and temptations test the mettle of our character. Gold and silver are refined by fire, and coal needs time and pressure to become

a strong beautiful diamond. Strength of character is shown not when all is well with our world, but in the presence of human pain and suffering. Take a look at a cup of hot chocolate covered with whip cream. We won't see what is in the bottom of our cup (heart) until someone bumps the cup (us) or permits suffering in our life. Without a doubt, I think the suffering that both Moses and the Israelites went through developed their character and gave them the strength to pursue the task God had intended for them, and it can do the same for us if we let it.

5.   **Pain loosens our grip on this life.** In time our work and our opinions are sought less and less. Our bodies become increasingly worse for the wear. Joints get sore, sleep gets difficult, memory fails us, and our overall health start to deteriorate. Problems seem larger and larger while options narrow. What went through the mind of the aged Moses as he ascended obediently up Mt. Nebo for the last time? If death is not the end but the threshold of a new day, then the curse of old age is also a blessing. Jesus said, " I go and prepare a place for you, and if I go and prepare a place for you, I will come back again, and take you to myself so that where I am you also may be."(John 14:3)

6.   **Suffering gives us a great opportunity to trust God.** God uses suffering that happens to us to bring us back, or to bring us closer to Him. Many times when an aliment comes upon us, we ask "Why me God?" I think this is a great opportunity not to ask why me, but to ask, what do you want me to do? When someone comes

down with cancer we ask the proverbial question why them or why me? We know for a fact that certain types of cancer are caused by smoking, and other forms of tobacco, too much exposure to sun etc. God didn't send it to us, but in many cases we have caused it by our own behavior, (smoking, chewing tobacco, or sun bathing too much). In many instances, we still don't know what causes many forms of cancers today and other diseases that afflict man. I am sure when we pay our research scientists as much as we pay our professional football and baseball players, we will get an answer to these questions. In the mean time, we have to trust in God. I strongly believe that Moses was left to conclude that if Yahweh had the power and wisdom to create this physical universe (as he knew it at that time), there was reason to trust this same God in times of suffering.

7. **God suffers with us in our suffering.** Yahweh conveys to Moses that He hears his people suffering. We sometimes ask ourselves if God is involved in the suffering of this world or is He indifferent to the suffering of this world. In the New Testament we see God talking to Saul on the road to Damascus, "Why are you persecuting me"? Yes, God does feel our suffering whether we realize it or not. He is not a cold God. No one has suffered like the One who paid for our sin in the crucified body of His own Son. Jesus knows what it is to be paralyzed, as He was paralyzed on the cross.

8. **God's comfort is greater than our own suffering.** When we have a loved one die, their pain stops, but our own pain continues with the grieving process. What we

should try to do is turn over this grieving to God and let Him carry it. God will take this grieving from you and give you the grace to endure. St. Paul pleaded with the Lord to take away an unidentified source of suffering. But God denied saying, "My grace is sufficient for you, for my strength is made perfect in weakness." The Book of Exodus is not a story about Moses weakness, but about God's strength. Moses learned that he would rather be with Yahweh in suffering than without God in good health and pleasant circumstances.

9. **People and families handle sickness and pain differently**. In times of crisis we find one another. Many times family members visit us who normally don't visit. It seems for some strange reason this crisis brings us closer together.

    Hurricanes, earthquakes, riots, illnesses, and even Egyptian Plagues all have a way of bringing us to our senses. Suddenly we remember our own mortality and that people are more important than things. In Moses outburst of anger He found out who he really was, and was afraid of what he saw. Each time we discover God's comfort in our own suffering, our capacity to help others is increased.

10. **God can turn suffering around for our good.** This truth is best seen in the many examples of the Bible. Through the rejection, betrayal, enslavement, and wrongful imprisonment of a man named Joseph, we see someone who eventually was able to say to those who had hurt him, "You meant evil against me; but God meant it for good" (Gen. 50:20). Many Jews were killed during

WWII, but yet this tragedy was turned around and a new country was born. In the history of mankind, we have attempted to make the world evil, but God meant the world to be good and intervened as he did with Pharaoh. God can turn suffering around to make it good. If you are ever looking for wisdom seek out someone who has suffered and kept his or her faith. This person will be well endowed with wisdom. God can turn our suffering around for our own good, if we only let Him.

In summation I would like to quote a brief part of a letter written by Pope John Paul II to the elderly on October 26, 1999. "The years pass quickly, and the gift of life, for all the effort and pain it involves, is too beautiful and precious for us ever to grow tired of it. We should stop to meditate on how quickly times flies, not in order to resign ourselves to an inexorable fate, but rather to make full use of the years we still have before us. These are years to be lived with a sense of trusting abandonment into the hands of God, our provident and merciful Father. It is a time to be used creatively for deepening our spiritual life through more fervent prayers and commitment to the service of our brothers and sister in charity".

MT. CARMEL - INTRODUCTION

Mount Carmel means vineyard of God from the Hebrew word Karem El. Some authors say it also means the beautiful garden land of God. Carmel is a mountain range of 14 miles the northwestern continuation of the hills of Samaria rising some 1600 ft above sea level. Most of the Carmel is covered with a thick deposit of good soil and abundant vegetation . The most outstanding biblical even that took place on Mt. Carmel was the triumphant victory of the prophet Elijah over the pagan prophets of Baal as found in 1 Kings.

Elijah the Tishbite was a fiery, rugged, powerful Hebrew prophet who feared no man. During his time, the Hebrew King Ahaz married a Phoenician (Lebanese) woman, Jezebel, who was a strong believer in the pagan god called Baal. King Ahaz built a temple for his wife's god and allowed pagan worship to spread in his land. Pagans believed that Baal was the master of the earth who controlled the weather and had the power to allow women to have children. In time, the ceremonies, which were sometimes, obscene, began to attract some of the Jews. The prophets of the Jews constantly denounced these ceremonies and Jezebel retaliated by killing these prophets. Elijah escaped and then challenged the prophets of Baal gathered on Mt. Carmel for a contest, which would determine once and for all which God – Baal or the Lord – was the true God. It was agreed that a prophet of Baal and a prophet of the Lord would each build a stone altar and place firewood and a sacrificial bull up on it. The God who would send fire from heaven upon the altar would be accepted as the "true God". Now we will read 1st King.

MT. CARMEL READING

1 Kings 18: 20-39 Ahab sent to all the Israelites and had the prophets assemble on Mount Carmel. Elijah appealed to all the people and said, "How long will you straddle the issue? If the Lord is God, follow him; if Baal, follow him." The people, however, did not answer him. So Elijah said to the people, "I am the only surviving prophet of the Lord, and there are four hundred and fifty prophets of Baal. Give us two young bulls. Let them choose one,

Mt. Carmel – The Prophet Elijah fought against the intentions of the queen Jezebel, wife of King Ahab, who tried to lead the people of Israel to forsake their belief in a single God in favor of the pagan god Baal.

cut it into pieces, and place it on the wood, but start no fire. I shall prepare the other and place it on the wood, but shall start no fire. You shall call on your gods, and I will call on the Lord. The God who answers with fire is God." All the people answered, "Agreed!" Elijah then said to the prophets of Baal, "Choose one young bull and prepare it first, for there are more of you. Call upon your gods but do not start the fire." Taking the young bull that was turned over to them, they prepared it and called on Baal from morning

*The false prophets pray in vain, while Elijah confidently
asks God to consume the sacrifice.*

to noon, saying, "Answer us, Baal!" But there was no sound, and
no one was answering. And they hopped around the altar they had
prepared. When it was noon, Elijah taunted them: "Call louder,
for he is good and may be meditating, or may have retired, or may
be on a journey. Perhaps he is asleep and must be awakened."
They called out louder and slashed themselves with swords and
spears, as was their custom, until blood gushed over them. Noon

passed and they remained in a prophetic state until the time for offering sacrifice. But there was not a sound; no one answered, and no one was listening. Then Elijah said to all the people, "Come here to me." When they had done so, he repaired the altar of the Lord, which had been destroyed. He took twelve stones, for the number of tribes of the sons of Jacob, to whom the Lord had said," Your name shall be Israel." He built an altar in honor of the Lord with the stones, and made a trench around the altar large enough for two seahs of grain. When he had arranged the wood, he cut up the young bull and laid it on the wood. "Fill four jars with water," he said, "and pour it over the holocaust and over the wood." Do it again," he said, and they did it again. "Do it a third time," he said, and they did it a third time. The water flowed around the altar, and the trench was filled with the water. At the time for offering sacrifice, the prophet Elijah came forward and said, "Lord, God of Abraham, Isaac, and Israel let it be known this day that You are God in Israel and that I am your servant and have done all these things by Your command. Answer me, Lord! Answer me, that this people may know that You, Lord, are God and that You have brought them back to their senses." The Lord's fire came down and consumed the holocaust, wood, stones, and dust, and it lapped up the water in the trench. Seeing this, all the people fell prostrated and said, "The Lord is God! The Lord is God!" Then Elijah said to them, "seize the prophets of Baal. Let none of them escape!" They were seized, and Elijah had them brought down to the brook Kishon and there he slit their throats.

REFLECTION

Elijah, the prophet asks the question, "How long will you (Israelites) straddle the issue?" Elijah was sent by God to convert the Israelites to worshiping the true God instead of Baal, a god of the pagans. In

Matthew's Gospel Jesus is speaking to Jews who think that if they follow him, they will have to give up the Torah as their living guide. However Jesus, as the new covenant, transcends the teachings of the Torah and offers a new relationship to the Torah. Jesus concern was to teach the people that the New Covenant, the kingdom of God, had arrived in their midst. What they are both calling us to is a commit- ment to the living God and to God's Son who steps beyond the Mosaic Law. May we all experience the power of Jesus as we face the challenge of taking a stand on issues that face us in the Church and in our society.

ALL SOULS DAY

Our Lady's promise to those who wear the brown scapular is this: Whosoever dies in this scapular shall not suffer eternal fire. On Saturday, as many as I shall find in Purgatory, I shall free," Blessed Calude de la Colombiere says that "of all the forms of our love for the Blessed Virgin and its various modes of expression, the scapular is the most favored." The prophecy of Ezechiel (Chap 46: 1-2) declares, "The gate of the inner court that looks toward the East shall be shut for six days, but on the Sabbath day it shall be opened." The Church has applied this prophecy to Our Lady of Mont Carmel. The "inner court" means Purgatory, and the "Sabbath day" means Saturday, the day when Our Lady abundantly release souls from Purgatory and brings them to Heaven.

THE BLESSING OF THE BROWN SCAPULARS

Priest: That you may have an outward sign and reminder of the giving and the acceptance, which is to take place today, we will bless and place over you the centuries-old sign of Carmelite dedication to Jesus, the Scapular of Our Lady of Mt. Carmel.

(place all the brown scapulars on the church altar, or have each person hold one over their arm)

Priest: Our help is in the name of the Lord.

All: Who made the heavens and the earth.

Priest: May the name of the Lord be blessed.

All: Now and forever.

Priest: Let us pray. Lord Jesus Christ, who so graciously assumed our human nature, we pray that You will continue to be generous with us, and bless (X) this (these) garments, made like those the Holy Father chose as an outward sign of humility, so that your servant who are about to wear it externally, may become more worthy and more aware that you are present internally. You who live and reign forever and ever.

All: Amen

The priest sprinkles the scapulars with holy water and then places one over the head of each person. What better place to become a member of the Confraternity of the brown scapular of Mt. Carmel than on Mt. Carmel. You may want to sing a Marian hymn in thanksgiving.

Enjoy the beautiful sight from Mt. Carmel and cherish the moment. These memories will last a life time. The pilgrimage is officially over now. Reflect on how God has bless you with speical graces througout this pilgrimage. We will return home soon as a changed person. Remember that the best is yet to come.

Chapter 10
Jaffa

The Gentiles are all called to be saved

Historical Note: The church dedicated to St. Peter, commemorates the events listed below. It was built between 1888 and 1894 on a part of the ancient citadel erected by Frederick II and restored by St. Louis, King of France at the beginning of the second half of the 13 century. The principal painting in the church depicts St. Peter on the roof of Simon the tanner's house, the event will be mentioned in detail below. Worth seeing is the pulpit, carved in the shape of a tree. Four panels in front show episodes in the life of St. Peter, namely the miraculous catch of fishes, the giving of the keys, the Transfiguration of Christ on Mt. Tabor, and the washing of the feet at the Last Supper. This is a great church to visit and read the below scriptures, but check first with the church as it closes between 12:00 noon and 2:00 PM.

Act of the Apostles 9: 36-43, 10: 1-48
Peter raises a woman to life at Jaffa.

At Jaffa there was a woman disciple called Tabitha, or Dorcas in Greek, who never tired of doing good or giving in charity. But the time came when she fell ill and died, and they washed her and laid her out in a room upstairs. Lydda is not far from Jaffa, when the disciple heard that Peter was there, they sent two men with an urgent message for him "Come and visit us as soon as possible." Peter went back with them straightaway, and on his arrival they took him to the upstairs room, where all the widows stood round him in tears, showing him tunics and other clothes Dorcas had made when she was with them. Peter sent them all out of the room and knelt down and prayed. Then he turned to the dead woman and said, "Tabitha, stand up". She opened her eyes, looked at Peter and sat up. Peter helped her to her feet, and then he called in the saints and widow and showed them she was alive. The whole of Jaffa heard about it and many believed in the Lord. Peter stayed on some time in Jaffa, lodging with a leather-tanner called Simon.

Peter Visits A Roman Centurion: One of the centurions who was stationed in Caesarea was called Cornelius. He and the whole of his household were devout and God-fearing and he gave generously to Jewish causes and prayed constantly to God. One day at about the ninth hour he had a vision in which he distinctly saw the angel of God come into his house and call out to him. Cornelius, he stared at the vision in terror and exclaimed. "What is it, Lord?" "Your offering of prayers and alms the angel answered, has been accepted by God. Now you must send someone to Jaffa and a fetch man called Simon, known as Peter, who is lodging with Simon the tanner, whose house is by the sea. When the angel who said this had gone, Cornelius called two of the slaves and a devout soldier of his staff, told them what had happened, and sent them off to Jaffa. Next day while they were still on their journey and had only a short distance to go before reaching Jaffa. Peter went to the housetop at about the sixth hour to pray. He felt hungry and was looking forward to his meal, but before it was ready he fell into a trance and saw heaven thrown open and something like a big sheet being let down to earth by its four corners; it contained every possible sort of animal and bird, walking, crawling or flying ones. A voice then said to him, "Now Peter: kill and eat!" But Peter answered, "Certainly not, Lord: I have never yet eaten anything profane or unclean". Again a second time, the voice spoke to him, "What God has made clean, and you have no right to call profane". This was repeated three times, and then suddenly the container was drawn up to heaven again. Peter was still worrying over the meaning of the vision he had seen, when the men sent by Cornelius arrived. They had asked where Simon's house was and they were now standing at the door, calling out to know if the Simon known as Peter was lodging there. Peter's mind was still on the vision and the Spirit had to tell him. Some men have come to see you. Hurry down, and do not hesitate about going back with them; it was I who told them to come. Peter went down and said to them, "I am the man you are looking for, why have you come?" They said, "the centurion Cornelius who is an upright and God-faring man, highly regarded by the entire Jewish people, was directed by a angel to send for you and bring you to his house and to listen to what you have to say". So Peter asked them in and gave them lodging. The next day, he was ready to go off with them, accompanied by some of the brothers from Jaffa. They reached Casarea the following day, and Cornelius was waiting for them. He had asked his relations and close friend to be there, and as Peter reached the house Cornelius went out to meet him, knelt at his feet and prostrated himself. But Peter helped him up, "Stand up", he said "I am only a man after all!" Talking together they went in to meet all the people assembled there, and Peter said to them, "You know it is forbidden for Jews to mix with people of

Jaffa – An ancient city several thousand years old, Jaffa already served in Biblical times as Jerusalem's seaport. St. Peter stayed in the house of Simon the Tanner before he went to Caesarea to baptize Cornelius.

another race and visit them, but God has made it clear to me that I must not call anyone profane or unclean. That is why I made no objection to coming when I was sent for, but I should like to know exactly why you sent for me". Cornelius replied " Three days ago I was praying in my house at the ninth hour, when I suddenly saw a man in front of me in shining robes. He said, "Cornelius, your prayer has been heard and your alms have been accepted as a sacrifice in the sight of God; so now you must send to Jaffa and fetch Simon known as Peter who is lodging in the house of Simon the tanner, by the sea." So I sent for you at once, and you have been kind enough to come. Here we all are, assembled in front of you to hear what message God has given you for us". Then Peter addressed them: "The truth I have now come to realize" he said "is that God does not have favorites, but that anybody of any nationality who fears God and does what is right is acceptable to Him.""It is true, God sent His word to the people of

Israel, and it was to them that the good news of peace was brought by Jesus Christ, but Jesus Christ is Lord of all men. You must have heard about the recent happening in Judaea: about Jesus of Nazareth and how he began in Galilee, after John had been preaching baptism. God had anointed Him with the Holy Spirit and with power, and because God was with Him. Jesus went about doing good, and curing all who had fallen into the power of the devil. Now I, and those with me, can witness to everything he did throughout the countryside of Judaea and in Jerusalem itself, and also to the fact that they killed Him by hanging Him on a tree, yet three days afterwards God raised Him to life and allowed him to be seen, not by the whole people but only by certain witnesses God has chosen beforehand. Now we are those witnesses.

REFLECTION

This reading is significant because it shows for the first time that God is calling Gentiles to follow him, not just the Jews. We see Peter praying for Tabitha. It was not his own power on which Peter called, it was the power of Jesus Christ. We think too much of what we can do and too little of what Christ can do through us. We see here a similarity between Peter and ourselves. It was at this point, which shows that Peter was already on the way to unlearning some of the rigidness in which he had been brought up with. I think we all have some rigidness we can get rid of in our own lives. You see Peter staying with a man call Simon who was a tanner. A tanner worked with the dead animals and skins of dead animals, therefore he was permanently unclean (Numbers 19: 11-13). No rigid Jew would have dreamed of accepting hospitality from a tanner. Once Peter would have called a Gentile unclean, but now God has prepared him for Cornelius. When Peter arrived at Caesarea, Cornelius met him at the door, no doubt wondering if Peter would cross his threshold at all, and Peter came in. In the most amazing way the barriers are beginning to go down. Let us step back and remember that the Jews believe at this time that others nations were quite outside the mercy of God. Even as Peter was speaking things began to happen against which even the Jewish Christians could not argue. The Spirit came upon Cornelius and his friends. They were lifted out of themselves in an ecstasy and began to speak with tongues. This to the Jews was the final proof of the astonishing fact that God had given his Spirit to the Gentiles too. Now you know the story.

PRAYER

Almighty Father, you are lavish in bestowing all Your gifts, and we give you thanks for the favors you have given us. In your goodness you have favored us and kept us safe in the past. We ask that you continue to protect us and to shelter us in the shadow of Your wings. We ask this though Christ our Lord. Amen

IMPORTANCE OF PRAYER-ROSARY IN OUR LIFE
(True Story That Was Never Told)

Most of us remember the time when Nikita Khrushchev visited the United Nations in October 1960, and boasted that they would bury us – would annihilate us! And to emphasize his boasting, he took off his shoe and pounded the desk before the horrified world assembly.

This was no idle boast, Khrushchev knew his scientists had been working on a nuclear missile and had completed their work and planned on November 1960, the 43rd anniversary of the Bolshevik Revolution, to present it to Khrushchev.

But here's what happened. Pope John XXIII had opened and

read the third Fatima secret given to Sister Lucy, He authorized the Bishop of Fatima to write to all the bishops of the world, inviting them to join with the pilgrims of Fatima on the night of October 12-13, 1960 in prayer and penance for Russia's conversion and consequent world peace.

On the night of October 12-13, about a million pilgrims spent the night outdoors in the Cova da Iria at Fatima in prayer and penance before the Blessed Sacrament. They prayed and watched despite a penetrating rain, which chilled them to the bone.

At the same time at least 300 dioceses throughout the world joined with them. Pope John XXIII sent a special blessing to all taking part in this unprecedented night of reparation.

Well, here is what happened. On the night between October 12-13, right after his shoe-pounding episode, Khrushchev suddenly pulled up stakes and few in all haste for Moscow, canceling all subsequent engagements. Why we ask?

Marshall Nedelin, and the best minds in Russia on nuclear energy and several government officials were present for the final testing of the missile that was going to be presented to Khrushchev. When the countdown was completed, the missile, for some reason or another, did not leave the launch pad. After waiting 15 or 20 minutes, Marshall Nedelin and all the others came out of shelter. When they did, the missile exploded killing over 300 people. This set back Russia's nuclear program for 20 years preventing all-out atomic warfare, and the burying of the United States. This all happened on the night when the whole Catholic world was on its knees before the Blessed Sacrament, gathered at the feet of our Lady, Queen of the Holy Rosary.

THE MEMORIES WILL LAST FOREVER!

The road to success is not always straight.
There is a curve called failures, a loop called
confusion, speed bumps called friends, red lights
called enemies, caution lights called family.
You will have flat tires called jobs. But if you have
a spare tire called determination, an engine called
perseverance, insurance called faith, and a driver called
Jesus, you will make it to a place called Success.

(Author Unknown)

*Christopher & Linda Cross in front of St. Patrick's Cathedral, NYC 1993
becoming members of the Knights of the Holy Sepulchre by Cardinal O'Connor.*

BIBLIOGRAPHY

Brownrigg, Ronald. Come, See The Place. London: Hodder and Stoughton, 1985.

Barclay, William, The Gospel of Matthew, Scotland, The Saint Andrew Press, 1975.

Bausch, William J. Pilgrim Church. CT. Twenty-Third Publications, 1998.

Bossa, Fr. Barry, S.A.C. Brown Scapular of Mt. Carmel, New Jersey, AMI Press, 1987

Corbo, Virgilio. The House Of St. Peter, Jerusalem: Franciscan Printing Press, 1972.

Enzler, Clarence J. My Other Self, New Jersey, Dimension Books, 1958.

Hill, Brennan, Jesus The Christ – Contemporary Perspectives, CT. Twenty-Third Publications, 2000.

Halaiko, David, The Holy Land, Nativity Press, Akron, Ohio, 1990

Huges, Bishop Alfred, Spiritual Masters, Indiana, Our Sunday Visitors Publishing, 1998.

Karris, Robert J. O.F.M. The Collegeville Bible Commentary The Liturgical Press, Minnesota 1992.

Kemp, Fr. Thomas, Daily Meditations, Ohio, Fairway Press, 1991

Kilgallen, John S.J. Guide to the Holy Land, Chicago, Loyola Press, 1998.

Marguerite, Message of Merciful Love To Little Souls, California, Pope Publications, 1981.

Murphy-O'Connor, Jerome. The Holy Land Archaeological Guide, Oxford University Press, 1986.

Nalbandian, Mardiros, Our Visit To The Holy Land, Jerusalem, Mount of Olives Press, 2000.

New American Bible, St. Joseph Edition, New York, Catholic Book Publishing Co. 1992.

The New Jerusalem Bible, Reader's Bible Edition, New York, Doubleday Publishing,1990.

Raymond, Fr. M. O.C.S.O. Spiritual Secrets of a Trappist Monk, New Hampshire, Sophia Press 2000

Rohr, Richard & Martos, Joseph, The Great Themes of Scripture, St. Anthony Messenger Press, 1987.

Shanks, Hershel, Ancient Israel – From Abraham to the Roman Destruction of the Temple, Biblical Archaeology Society, 1999.

Sieracki, Fr. Aloysius, O.Carm. Carmel's Call, Illinois, The Carmelite Press 1991.

Vanderwall, Francis W. Freedom From Fear, Louisiana, Acadian House Publishing 1999.

Vaux, Roland de, O.P. Ancient Israel, William Eerdmans Publishing Co, Michigan 1997

Wiekerkehr, Macrina, O.S.B. Seasons of Your Heart, New York, Harper-Collins Publishing, 1991.

INDEX

PRAYER AT THE END
OF OUR PILGRIMAGE

Father, we have walked in the land where Jesus walked. We have touched the soil and rocks where the seed falls. We have seen the lillies of the field and heard the birds of the air. We have been warmed by the sun that warmed Him, and cooled by the breezes that touched His face. We have been to the sea where He walked, and to the river where He was baptized. We have felt the presence of the Holy Spirit where He first sent it, and anguished at the spot where He gave Himself for us. We have rejoiced at the emptiness of His tomb and the fullnes of His love in our Hearts. Be with us as we continue our earthly pilgrimage to the New Jerusalem where every tear will be wiped away and we will be with You, Your Son and the Holy Spirit forever. Amen

"If I forget you, O Jerusalem, may my right hand be forgotten."

St. Francis Prayer

Lord, make me an instument of Your peace. Where there is hatred, let me sow love, Where there is injury, pardon. Where there is doubt, faith. Where there is despair, hope. Where there is darkness, light. And where there is sadness, joy. O Divine Master, grant that I may not so much seek to be consoled as to console; to be understood as to understand; to be loved as to love. For it is in giving that we receive, it is in pardoning that we are pardoned, and it is in dying that we are born to eternal life.